WHAT PEOPLE ARE SAYING

LIVE BIG will fill your sails with thoughtful practical tips, wise mental health habits, and, most importantly, the unbridled optimism that every entrepreneur needs to forge ahead. If you're thinking about ways to make a bigger impact with more joy, this is a must read! I couldn't put it down and felt re-energized. I loved feeling Stacey's bright light shine through every page.

—Margot Schmorak
CEO and Co-Founder of Hostfully
Co-Founder of VC-Backed Moms Community

A beautiful book with no "fluff." Anyone who reads this and knows Stacey will know this all truly came from her heart. *LIVE BIG* isn't just another self-help book. It's literally a saving grace for those who will take it, trust it, and roll with it.

—Brenna Carles
CEO and Founder at The Mortgage Shop

LIVE BIG is the perfect blend of heartfelt wisdom and actionable strategies that every entrepreneur needs. Stacey's passion and authenticity jump off the pages, making this more than just a book— it's a life-changing guide. It's packed with powerful insights that will inspire you to dream bigger, act smarter, and approach your journey with renewed energy and confidence. If you're ready to transform both your mindset and your business, this is a must-have.

—Avery Carl
CEO and Founder, The Short Term Shop

As a passionate advocate for personal and professional growth, I cannot emphasize enough how transformative Stacey St. John's *LIVE BIG* book is. Stacey masterfully distills complex concepts into actionable principles that resonate deeply with both seasoned entrepreneurs and those just starting their journey. The insights shared in *LIVE BIG* have the potential to revolutionize the way you approach challenges, cultivate relationships, and harness your unique strengths.

The principles outlined in this book encourage us to step beyond our comfort zones and embrace the possibilities that come with Living BIG—both personally and professionally. If you're ready to unlock your potential and transform your business, I wholeheartedly recommend diving into *LIVE BIG*. It's an investment in yourself and your future that will pay dividends beyond measure.

—**Monica Scalf**
Founder, The Work Well Group

LIVE BIG is a game-changer for entrepreneurs ready to unlock growth in themselves and their business—while creating a life that truly aligns with their dreams. Stacey St. John masterfully combines practical resources, powerful stories, and transformative exercises to help you break through roadblocks and build not just a financially successful business, but also a life filled with joy and purpose. Her strategies are refreshingly simple, actionable, and designed to be implemented right away, providing a clear path to achieving meaningful results. This book is a must-read for anyone who is ready to stop playing small and step into their full potential.

—**Valerie Malone**
Owner, Quill Decor

Stacey has an incredible gift for helping you shift your perspective and see the light beyond your limiting beliefs. Her wisdom cuts through the noise of self-doubt and brings clarity, revealing the truth of who you are meant to be.

LIVE BIG is more than a book; with real-world examples, it acts as a guide for women ready to break free, grow, and embrace their fullest potential. I highly recommend it to anyone who wants to overcome self-imposed barriers and step boldly into the life they were created to live.

—**Alicia Wright**
Owner, Blue Palm Getaways

LIVE
BIG

AN ENTREPRENEUR'S PLAYBOOK TO BOSS UP
YOUR BUSINESS, SHOW UP FOR YOURSELF,
AND STEP INTO YOUR DREAM LIFE

STACEY ST. JOHN

LIVE BIG
An Entrepreneur's Playbook to Boss Up Your Business, Show Up for Yourself, and Step into Your Dream Life

For permission requests, speaking inquiries, and bulk order purchase options, visit LiveBigWithStacey.com.

Photography by Lauren Difulvio
Editing by Lori Lynn Enterprises
Design by Transcendent Publishing | TranscendentPublishing.com

ISBN: 979-8-9918968-1-8

Disclaimer: The information provided in this book is for educational and informational purposes only. While it offers strategies and insights to help you achieve success, no specific financial or income results are guaranteed. Your results will depend on various factors, including your effort, dedication, and individual circumstances. The author and publisher make no representations or warranties regarding financial outcomes as a result of using the methods and strategies outlined in this book.

"The biggest adventure you can ever take
is to live the life of your dreams."

—Oprah Winfrey

CONTENTS

For Mom, who taught me that life
is too short not to enjoy it.

FOREWORD

In a world overflowing with entrepreneurial advice and self-help literature, it's rare to find a gem that can not only capture the essence of transformative change but also radiate with genuine passion and practical wisdom. Stacey St. John's *LIVE BIG* is that rare gem. As someone who has seen the transformative power of Stacey's insights and principles firsthand, I am both honored and thrilled to pen the foreword for this inspiring guide.

Stacey has long been a beacon of support and encouragement, particularly for women navigating the entrepreneurial landscape. As a stalwart cheerleader for women in business, especially within the Short-Term Rental industry, Stacey has dedicated herself to lifting others up and championing their success. Her relentless drive and unwavering belief in the capabilities of women are vividly reflected in the pages of this book.

Through her remarkable journey, Stacey has transformed her life from the confines of a corporate grind to the exhilarating heights of entrepreneurial success. Her transformation to a dynamic entrepreneur running a thriving business, whilst maintaining a lifestyle envious of others, is a powerful illustration of what is possible when one dares to dream big and take decisive action. In LIVE BIG, she doesn't just share her story; she extends a hand to guide others along a similar path. Her insights are grounded in real experiences, and her strategies are practical and actionable.

One of the most compelling aspects of Stacey's approach is her ability to inspire confidence and action. As she aptly puts it in her book, "Unleash your inner badass."

These words are more than a catchphrase—they are a call to action, a reminder that within each of us lies the power to break free from self-imposed limitations and achieve greatness. Stacey's own journey is a testament to this very principle.

Her message is clear and powerful: "Be a champion, not a critic." In a world where self-doubt and negativity can often overshadow our potential, Stacey encourages us to embrace a mindset of positivity and self-belief. This empowering philosophy is at the heart of LIVE BIG, providing a roadmap for anyone looking to overcome obstacles and achieve their dreams.

As a friend and admirer of Stacey, I have witnessed firsthand the transformative impact she has on those around her. Her unwavering support, infectious enthusiasm, and genuine desire to see others succeed are qualities that make her not just a mentor but a true inspiration. I am incredibly proud of her ever-evolving impact and the countless lives she has touched through her work and her friendship.

LIVE BIG is not merely a guide; it is a celebration of the potential within each of us to craft lives that are both successful and deeply fulfilling. Stacey St. John has poured her heart and soul into this book, and I am confident that her insights will resonate with you as they have with me. Her wisdom, passion, and dedication make this book an invaluable resource for anyone ready to take bold steps toward a life of purpose and achievement.

It is my pleasure to commend this book to you, and I am confident that it will inspire and empower you to take the next steps toward your own extraordinary future.

—**Julie George**
Author, Business Coach, Million Dollar Host
milliondollarhost.com.au

FROM SELF-DOUBT TO LIVING BIG

I was stuck on a hamster wheel, feeling like I was going nowhere. My six-figure job, once a source of pride, started to feel more like a ball and chain than a blessing, weighing me down. The "healthy" salary I worked so hard for was costing me more than just time—it was costing me my freedom.

My alarm would blare at 4 a.m., and I'd trudge to the kitchen, desperate for my first cup of coffee before diving into the daily grind. Leading the sales division for a global organization meant my inbox was always overflowing, and requests from clients in every time zone were relentless.

After a few hours of early morning work, I'd hit the shower at 7 a.m., head out the door for the office at 7:45, and endure a traffic-clogged 45-minute commute filled with phone calls to colleagues in Europe and Asia. Then, I'd be at my desk by 8:30, ready to "officially" start my workday.

Eight hours in the office, another traffic-filled drive home, and more work before heading into the kitchen to fix dinner. After a quick meal and cleaning up the dishes, I'd crash into bed, utterly exhausted.

I dreamt about leaving my W2, but the golden handcuffs dug in deep. I'd started investing in real estate a few years prior. New ideas about living off my real estate income sparked excitement in me, but the self-doubt monster would constantly rear its ugly head.

It whispered, "You don't have the funds to buy enough properties to make that happen yet."

I kept telling myself, "You'll have to just stick it out for a while longer," even though deep down, I craved more—to spend my days doing something I truly loved, something that made me feel alive and fulfilled.

I started dreaming about businesses I could build around my passions. But every time I'd start to envision a better future, that self-doubt monster would shut down my ideas faster than I could even blink.

The fear of failure was real. It felt like a suffocating blanket wrapped tightly around me. As a prisoner of my own mind and crazy schedule, I kept pushing aside my dreams, ignoring the potential I wasn't tapping into.

At my job, the weight of the world seemed to rest on my shoulders, and with each passing month and year, my stress level intensified. I felt like a tightrope walker, balancing on a thin wire of sanity, desperate not to fall.

On the outside, I wore a mask of composure for my colleagues, friends, and family—a brittle smile that concealed the growing emptiness inside me. But the cracks were beginning to show to those closest to me.

One Sunday morning, my husband's concern pierced me like an arrow through the heart. "Honey," his voice was gentle, "you seem so distant. Is everything okay?"

The question hung in the air. And then, as if a dam had burst, the tears came. A torrent of raw emotion poured out of me, and one of those good ol' ugly cries unleashed. The words tumbled out, a jumbled mess of frustration and despair as I sobbed.

Once I was able to regain control of myself, I poured my heart out, confessing how work had morphed into a bleak, monotonous grind. I was a ghost, going through the motions, numb and exhausted. Life had become a relentless blur, leaving no space for me.

I longed for something different, to do work that ignited my passions and fueled my soul. But the path forward was shrouded in fog. All I knew was that I wanted to get back the joy and laughter that had once filled my days.

In that vulnerable moment, it hit me hard: I had been a passenger in my own life, letting life just happen to me instead of taking the wheel.

It was time to take control of my future and chart a new course, starting with a transformation of myself. I realized I didn't need permission to chase my dreams. I just needed to unlock the secrets of attracting the life I truly craved.

The next day, with a newfound determination burning bright, I wiped away my tears and plunged into the unknown. The next twelve months became a whirlwind of self-discovery. Yep, I was still up at 4 a.m., but instead of doing work for my corporate gig,

I was working on me, learning to silence my self-doubt and start believing in the person staring back in the mirror every morning.

I devoured books, articles, and podcasts, desperate to understand the intricate workings of my mind and how to rewire it for success. It was like uncovering a hidden treasure map to my own potential. I experimented with new habits, stacking small wins into a mountain of progress. And with each breakthrough, I felt a surge of exhilaration, propelling me faster toward the freedom I craved.

One step at a time, I chipped away at the limitations holding me back, and I turned my real estate investing "side gig" into a revenue-generating machine. In two years, I took $50K and turned it into a $2 million real estate portfolio.

A year into my entrepreneurial journey, the once seemingly impenetrable corporate cage shattered into pieces. I stood tall, a transformed woman, CEO of my own destiny. With a heart full of gratitude, a thriving real estate portfolio, and six months' worth of savings in the bank, I traded in my W2 for the freedom to pursue my passions.

June 30, 2022, marked the day I stepped into a new chapter, waking up each morning excited to live a life I'd always dreamed of and earning paychecks fueled by my passions. I was 48 years old, starting a brand new career, and walking away from the comfort of my W2.

Was it scary? Heck yeah.

Did other people think I was crazy? You bet.

But I'd never been so darned excited to be afraid and have other people call me nuts!

You see, it didn't matter what other people thought. I'd learned how to believe in myself.

It didn't matter that I felt scared. I'd learned how to push through fear.

It didn't matter that I was 48 and felt like I was starting over. I had finally learned that life is way too short not to live it fully and enjoy every moment.

I share my story not to boast, but as a beacon of hope. Because I know what it feels like to be trapped in a life that doesn't ignite your soul.

Whether you're reading this at age 28, 48, or 68, you deserve to have everything you dream of, and it's *never* too late for a reset.

I want you to know that the key to unlocking your extraordinary potential already lies within you. Maybe you're trapped in the daily grind, a hamster wheel of monotony. Or perhaps a brilliant business idea is simmering on the back burner, waiting for its moment to shine. It could be that you've already built something incredible but find yourself drained and yearning for more.

I understand. Because I've been there, too.

But I'll let you in on a little secret: that entrepreneurial rock star you suspect is buried somewhere inside? She's not a figment of your imagination. She's real and waiting to break free. And I'm here to help you unleash that powerhouse within.

Who Is Stacey St. John?

I'm a regular midwestern wife and mom with a love for fun and a deep belief that God has a plan for each of us. I've achieved some pretty cool things in life, but trust me, I've faced plenty of self-doubt, second guessing, and overwhelm along the way.

My husband always says I can do anything I set my mind to, and you know what? He's right. But let me tell you, reaching the goals I've set for myself takes real work. It's not always easy, and my life is far from perfect. However, I choose to see every mistake, failure, or bump in the road as a lesson, a chance to level up and become the best version of myself. And I put my mind to work *for me* in everything I do. I no longer just leave results up to chance.

Take my *Wheel of Fortune* appearance in 2013—that wasn't pure luck. I'd actually auditioned years before and struck out. But I didn't give up. I auditioned again, made it onto the show, and then studied letter patterns until the cows came home. I couldn't control what my fellow contestants did on the show, but I could control how well I knew letter sequences. The result? I walked away from my time on the show with $27,000 and a trip to St. Croix.

The same goes for winning the Sweet Adelines International Quartet Championship twice. Those trophies weren't sprinkled with pixie dust. My quartet and I poured countless hours into practice, rising from unranked to world champions in just a few short years.

Since 2022, I've built the top training and mentoring program for women in the short-term rental industry. But let me assure you, I didn't just become an "Airbnb Queen" overnight. It took relentless dedication to build a thriving real estate and hospitality business that benefits both my family and my clients. Now, I teach others how to do the same.

Look, I'm not sharing this to make myself seem special. The truth is, the key to success is staring at me every morning—she's right there in my mirror. And guess what? She's in your mirror, too.

There's no quick fix, no magic pill you can take to instantly create the life of your dreams. The truth is, the transformation happens when you're willing to do the hard work—on yourself. The moment you realize **you** hold the key to your dream life, that's when your world truly begins to change. And guess what? I'm here to be your guide and your biggest cheerleader every step of the way.

Ready to LIVE BIG?

Let this book be your wake-up call to ditch the excuses you're telling yourself and step into the spotlight of your own dreams. "Living BIG" isn't about chasing some pre-fabricated version of success—it's about crafting a business and a life that ignites your soul.

Forget the whispers of self-doubt that tell you to "play it safe." I'm living proof that becoming a person of action, learning how to make strategic choices every day, and embracing all the bumps along the way is key to unlocking your full potential.

I've achieved incredible things, but it all started with a simple decision to stop comparing myself to others, ditch my doubts, believe in myself, and start chasing my own vision.

LIVE BIG is your roadmap to pushing past limitations and achieving what once seemed impossible. You'll learn to leave the comparisons at the door and replace them with unshakeable confidence. You'll learn to make impactful decisions based on your passions and goals, and unleash the rock star entrepreneur who's been waiting to burst out.

This book is packed with practical tools to create a business and a life that fuels your fire, not just your to-do list. And, yes, you *can* have both.

Are you ready to stop being a spectator in your own life and start living BIG?

Let's embark on this adventure together. We'll shatter the limitations of comparison and turn those impossible dreams into your everyday reality.

Your greatness is waiting. Let's unleash it together.

CHAPTER 1

BOSS² UP, SHOW UP, AND STEP UP

There comes a moment when you realize you've been living for everyone else—driving the kids around, keeping the house in order, and hitting deadlines for your boss—while your own passions and dreams take a back seat. You have zero focus on what *truly* fuels your soul.

Maybe you're starting to feel that at this point in your life, or maybe you've been stuck there for a while. Well, things are about to change for you.

Let me introduce you to the LIVE BIG framework, a powerful approach I created to help you stop living on autopilot and start designing a life that excites you, aligns with your passions, and allows you to pursue your biggest dreams with confidence and purpose.

By shifting your habits, your thinking, and your hustle, you can go from being a passive passenger to being in the driver's seat of your own life. Think of it as your personal roadmap to becoming the rock star entrepreneur you were always meant to be. But this isn't just about building a business; it's about crafting a life that fuels your deepest passions and sets your spirit ablaze.

This framework is built on what I learned along the way during my own personal transformation: practical strategies, proven mindset shifts, and the systems I used to turn my life around and scale a real estate portfolio from $50K to $2 million—while keeping joy front and center in my life, regardless of all the challenges that bubbled up.

The LIVE BIG framework isn't about taking baby steps; it's about playing full-out to create the life you deserve. You're reading this book because you don't want to just get by—you're ready to thrive—and this framework will show you how to do it, one bold move at a time.

From this moment on, ditch being the passenger in your life. It's time to get in the driver's seat and actively shape your destiny. Repeat it with me: "I am a person of action, and I am Living BIG!"

The 3 Principles of the LIVE BIG Framework

Let's explore the three core principles that form the foundation of the LIVE BIG framework. They will act as your compass, guiding you toward a life of fulfillment and success on your terms.

PRINCIPLE 1: Boss^2 Up

Chart Your Course to Greatness

You wake up every morning energized by a clear vision, knowing exactly where you're headed and how to get there. That's the power of Bossing Up! Your **B**ehaviors are focused on your **O**utcomes, and you use **S**trategy, **S**kills, & **S**ystems (**Boss**^{2}) to map out a step-by-step plan to achieve them. Whether your dream is a 7-figure business or conquering that hour-long meeting with confidence, when you Boss^2 Up, you'll have clarity and an action plan to forge ahead with laser focus.

PRINCIPLE 2: Show Up

Own Your Power and Purpose

Showing up isn't about perfection. (Because, let's face it, who's perfect?) It's about committing to being your best self in every aspect of your life. You prioritize your well-being, intentionally choose how to spend your time, and focus on work that fuels your passion. You understand how your mind operates and how to get your brain to work *for* you. And you radiate confidence and attract opportunities that align perfectly with your values.

PRINCIPLE 3: Step Up

Make Tough Choices and Embrace Challenges

Comfort zones are comfortable, but you understand that true growth happens when you face challenges and fears head-on. You embrace calculated risks, knowing that setbacks are just stepping stones, not roadblocks. You understand that taking bold leaps leads to the most rewarding experiences, and you accept that detours are part of the journey. When failures happen (and they will), you choose to fail forward and keep moving.

How to Turn Visions Into Victories

You know the feeling. You've got these incredible ideas swirling around in your mind and a burning desire to break through your glass ceiling and take your business to the next level. But then reality hits.

Your day-to-day takes over.

Back-to-back meetings, customer issues to solve, and a to-do list that feels endless. Days turn into weeks, and before you know it, those ideas that once lit you up are buried under the weight of it all.

Here's the secret weapon you've been missing: **alignment.**

This alignment isn't just a fancy concept—it's the difference between spinning your wheels and experiencing the thrill of meaningful progress. Imagine waking up each day energized by tasks that directly contribute to achieving your biggest dreams. That's the Boss^2 Up magic!

When your behaviors are aligned with your desired outcomes, your daily hustle doesn't feel like a chore; it becomes a purposeful march toward building the business (and the life) you envision.

Why is alignment so powerful? When you Boss^2 Up, you're not just chasing goals aimlessly. You become a strategist, architecting a roadmap to success. And this roadmap outlines the key areas you need to focus on to get to the next level while giving you an easy-to-follow system that keeps you on track. It's like having a personal GPS for your goals and dreams, ensuring you never lose sight of your next step.

By aligning your daily actions with your desired outcomes, you'll transform from a visionary into a progress-maker, moving forward one purposeful step at a time. So, let's Boss^2 Up and turn your dreams into reality!

Here's what it looks like:

- **B = Behaviors**—the actions you take
- **O = Outcomes**—the amazing goals, dreams, and desires you want to achieve
- **S = Strategy**—your awesome plan to bring your outcomes to life
- S^2 = the **Skills & Systems** needed to execute your plan

Let me tell you about a turning point in my journey, where "goal setting" took on a whole new meaning for me. I was on the leadership team for a global consulting firm, and we were implementing Gino Wickman's Entrepreneurial Operating System (EOS®) into our business. Each week, we'd review our quarterly goals and break them down into clear, actionable tasks for each of us to tackle over the next seven days.

The following week, we'd repeat the process, always refining and executing. It felt like a roadmap continuously unfolding, each step chosen with purpose to propel us toward our collective dream.

What I learned from this experience is the true power of alignment—how turning big visions into focused, weekly actions can create unstoppable momentum. It taught me that success doesn't happen by chance; it happens by design.

Fast forward a few years, and this same philosophy became the cornerstone of Kozy Getaways, my vacation rental management business. Here, the big, audacious goal? Hitting a cool $1 million in revenue.

The moment I launched the business, I started holding weekly leadership team meetings—even though the only one on the team was "me, myself, and I." That's right! I set time aside to meet with myself, review my goals, measure my progress, and create action steps to build the infrastructure, systems, and processes needed to support a million-dollar operation. It wasn't just about checking off tasks—it was about laying the foundation for a scalable, sustainable business from the ground up.

Did it work? You bet! In our second year, we blew past that million-dollar mark, bringing in an incredible $1,244,167 in revenue. But seeing that number on the financial report didn't come as a surprise. Why? Because the $1 million goal was always front and center, guiding every decision and every action. I wasn't just grinding—I was building a business with intention, designed to grow and thrive.

And here's the thing: this Boss[2] Up approach works with *any* desired outcome you want to work on—whether you want to travel the world, become a black belt in karate, or learn a foreign language. The key is harnessing the power of your vision, letting it fuel your actions and transform your goals into reality. That's the magic I want to share with you in this book.

Real Quick, Let's Talk Zones

So, you're ready to crush your goals? That's amazing! But before we go any further, let's talk about your **Comfort Zone**. Stepping outside of it isn't easy, and the moment you do, you'll find yourself in the **Fear Zone**. That's when that little voice inside your head will start whispering, "I'm not cut out for this. This is just too much work. Why does everything have to be so hard?" Suddenly, you're tempted to retreat back to safety.

But here's the truth about that temptation. It's actually a sign that you're on the path to growth. By leaning into the discomfort and embracing those fears, you'll soon step into the **Learning Zone**— and eventually, the **BIG Zone**, where you're consistently operating at full potential and living a life filled with joy and purpose.

Right now, I want you to commit to embracing change, even when it feels scary. It's a secret ingredient to unleashing your inner rock star and blossoming into your most powerful self.

The Adventure Begins

Now that you have the three pillars of the LIVE BIG framework, you know the importance of alignment, and you're committed to stepping outside your Comfort Zone, you're ready to embark on the journey of a lifetime.

In the following chapters, we'll dive deeper into each principle of the LIVE BIG framework. But first, let me be clear about an important point. This book is not intended to be another self-help book that collects dust on your shelf. This is your playbook for action, and each chapter is designed to help you take real, meaningful steps toward living your best life.

So don't just read. Implement what you learn.

And as you turn to the next page, make the decision to show up for yourself. Commit to taking action and get ready to see what's truly possible when you embrace the power of Living BIG. Let's dive in!

CHAPTER 2

A CBD CAUTIONARY TALE

F orget everything you think you know about CBD. This isn't about calming down your anxious cat or treating your sore muscles. This CBD is a different kind of remedy—a cure for the uninspired, the stuck, and the "I-wish-I-could-but-I-can't" mentality.

This CBD stands for Commit, Be, Do. It's a triple-threat formula for taking your dreams and turning them into reality. Buckle up, because this chapter injects a powerful dose of "get-it-done" into your system.

Why "Have-Do-Be" Can Sink Your Success Story

Let's imagine that you're a real estate investor, and you've meticulously crafted the perfect vacation rental empire. Guests rave about your charming beach bungalows and rustic mountain cabins. Bookings are flooding in, and you're feeling like the next real estate mogul, basking in the glow of your success.

Then, seemingly out of nowhere, reality swoops in and shows you that your "perfect" plan isn't so perfect after all.

Enter Allie, a superstar student in my STR Success Accelerator & Achievers Club programs. (Don't worry, I changed her name to protect her privacy.) Allie's story is a masterclass in the perils of the "Have-Do-Be" approach—a philosophy that trips up countless entrepreneurs before they even hit their stride.

Here's the "Have-Do-Be" trap in action: Allie, fueled by pure passion, went into hyper-growth mode. She snapped up properties, dabbled in rental arbitrage (think building an Airbnb empire from properties you rent, not own), and even managed bookings for other Airbnb hosts.

Impressive, right? Not quite.

Allie unknowingly built her success on an unstable foundation. Imagine a dream vacation rental business teetering on the edge of legal quicksand—that's the risk Allie took by neglecting to set up a proper legal structure for her business from the get-go. Her financial stability was unknowingly at risk because she hadn't created an entity structure that protected her personal assets.

Her rental agreements with guests were shaky at best, and she was completely dependent on Airbnb for bookings—a single platform that can suspend your listing in an instant (and trust me, it happens more often than you'd think!). This meant her revenue could disappear overnight if something went wrong.

Even her co-hosting clients—Airbnb owners she supported—weren't exactly ideal partners, and she didn't have proper agreements in place. The risk? They could cut ties at a moment's notice, leaving her with no way to recoup commissions on future bookings she had worked so hard to secure.

Here's the core of the issue: Allie believed she needed to *have* a certain level of success first—a thriving, top-performing Airbnb portfolio and a roster of co-hosting clients. Only then, she thought, could she *do* the work of building a strong foundation and finally *be* the CEO of a rock-solid business.

The problem? By the time we connected, Allie was drowning in the "fixing" stage.

Building a sustainable business required a tough course correction. Allie scaled back her portfolio, letting go of clients who didn't value her expertise. She started setting up an entity structure to safeguard her family's financial future, but untangling her business felt like a never-ending project.

She took a hit in profitability. Lawyers aren't cheap, and a smaller portfolio meant less revenue. Doesn't exactly feel like the most energizing entrepreneurial journey, right?

Imagine the frustration, the lost time and money—all because Allie subscribed to the "Have-Do-Be" fallacy.

By flipping the script to "Commit-Be-Do," Allie could have built a solid foundation from day one.

Committing to her desired outcomes from the start would have meant she'd be the person that prioritizes diversified revenue streams (a characteristic of a successful business). And she'd do what's necessary to list her properties on multiple sites, not relying on a single online travel platform. The result of CBD in this instance? Less risk and less stress.

This commitment would've also meant she'd be focusing on building a rock-solid entity structure to protect her finances early on, and she'd do what's necessary to keep that veil of protection. The result of CBD here? Less risk and less stress.

Had Allie followed the CBD approach, she would've committed to cultivating strong client relationships from the get-go, and would be the person who has solid agreements in place. What would CBD mean here? Less risk and less stress.

Eh hem … are you sensing a theme in these results?

And, lastly, had Allie followed the CBD approach, she would've had the energy and focus to do what truly matters in a hospitality-focused business, which is creating unforgettable experiences for her guests. What would her results have been? Better reviews and higher income.

In these scenarios alone, the "Commit-Be-Do" approach would've reduced her risk, lowered her stress, improved her reviews, and boosted her revenue.

Get the drift?

So, why don't most people operate in CBD mode? Well, often, it's a long-standing belief system that needs to be adjusted (we'll walk through that in future chapters).

What I want you to do now, though, is commit to avoiding the trap of these limiting beliefs. Commit to operating like the badass boss lady you are, and forget waiting for some magical moment of "having" to arrive before you start "doing" and "being" the person you were meant to be.

By flipping the script and embracing "Commit-Be-Do," you become the architect of your success story, not a character reacting to circumstances.

Imagine for a moment that you're the CEO of your dream business empire. You're focused on growth, not scrambling to fix cracks in a wobbly foundation. Confidently, you make strategic decisions that propel you toward long-term success.

A Quick Word About Commitment

When we LIVE BIG, we also need to remove words from our vocabulary. The first word we're going to remove is the word "try."

Let's get one thing straight—there's a world of difference between **trying** to do something and **committing** to do it.

Commitment isn't just a mindset; it's a roadmap. It keeps you focused, provides direction, and fuels your motivation. Even when the going gets tough, commitment ensures you're ready to put in the time, sweat, and resources to get to your endgame. It's the secret sauce to staying consistent and dedicated.

Unwavering commitment is your trusty shield against obstacles and your ticket through hard times. It's your building blocks of discipline and consistency, forming a routine and structure that's vital for progress.

Every journey to improvement has its bumps, but being unwavering helps you build the resilience and determination to keep going. It keeps you positive, reminding you of the grand plan and the rewards that await.

The beauty of CBD? It's a life-changing formula.

Dreaming of a million-dollar business? Commit to yourself right now. Be the leader of that 7-figure powerhouse. Why postpone those next-level choices?

Start "doing" today what a successful CEO does. Make decisions with a millionaire mindset. Build a network that fuels your success. Structure your time like a well-oiled machine.

The CBD operating approach isn't just applicable to your business—it works wonders in your personal life, too!

Ever crave a clutter-free desk, but feel like you're constantly battling piles of papers and post-it notes?

The key isn't waiting for a magically organized workspace to appear. It's flipping the script!

Commit to "being" an organized person—right now.

Imagine yourself, the organized whiz you've always wanted to be. Picture your workspace as a clutter-free haven, where everything has its place. The best part? It only takes a few minutes a day. Become a filing pro and conquer your day with laser focus—all from the comfort of your organized oasis.

And keep in mind, a daily tidy-up isn't just a chore, it's a building block. You're training your brain, forming the habits of an organized person.

When you commit to being organized, the actions of an organized person start to come naturally. It becomes easier and easier to do the things that keep you on track.

You'll find yourself naturally gravitating toward putting things away, and that picture-perfect office transforms from just a dream to your reality.

Want to be a confident public speaker? Start acting like one. Research relentlessly, rehearse with passion, and envision yourself captivating the audience. The more you practice being the confident speaker, the more the "doing" becomes second nature, and stage fright fades away.

Ditch the "have-to" mentality and embrace the CBD revolution. First, commit to being the person you want to become, and then watch your actions and your life transform around you!

Forget Waiting in the Wings, It's Time to Take Center Stage!

How do we infuse ourselves with unshakeable dedication to our goals? Let's break it down step-by-step, with a sprinkle of real talk and a whole lot of "you've got this!"—because you absolutely do!

Step 1: Unearth Your Inner What & Why

What sets your soul on fire, and why? What do you want your business to achieve, and why? Is it financial freedom? Why does that matter to you? Do you want to make a difference in the world? Why is that a priority for you? Write it down, pin it to your mirror, shout it from the rooftops if you have to! Clarity on your "what" and "why" is the foundation of unshakable commitment.

Here's an important tip: make sure your "why" is tied to more than just money. Connect it to something that brings you true joy, something that makes you feel fulfilled. That's where the real magic happens.

**Step 2: Be Your Own Cheerleader
(Because Self-Doubt Is a Dud)**

Now's the time to kick some serious butt in your life! But let's be real. Self-doubt has a way of showing up uninvited. And you know what? That's okay! It's completely normal.

The key is to acknowledge it, then drown it out with your inner cheerleader. Celebrate every win, big or small. Did you finally stick to your morning routine for a week? Do a victory dance!

Did you push through that workout when you almost quit? High-five yourself! Did you make time for a family dinner after a crazy day? Jump for joy!

And celebrate your business wins with gusto, too! Hit a new sales target? Treat yourself! Launched a killer marketing campaign? Do a happy dance on your desk!

Celebrating and believing in yourself is like a muscle—the more you flex it, the stronger it gets. Treat each accomplishment like the victory it is. Self-doubt may sneak in, but the more you show up for yourself and celebrate the progress, the louder that inner cheerleader gets. So keep flexing, because you're building something amazing!

Step 3: Embrace the Journey

The road to success, like anything worth having, won't always be sunshine and rainbows. There will be bumps, detours, and moments where you just want to hide under the covers. But I can promise you this: the journey is full of incredible rewards. Focus on your progress, learn from your setbacks, and use those challenges as stepping stones to come back even stronger.

Think about the devastation of a forest fire. What seems destructive at first is actually clearing the way for new growth, making the forest healthier and more vibrant than ever. Your setbacks are simply preparing you for greater success.

Step 4: Find Your Tribe (Because Entrepreneurship Can Be Lonely)

Surround yourself with other badasses who get you. Find mentors, join networking groups, or build a squad of cheerleaders who will lift you up when you wobble. Sharing your journey with supportive, like-minded people amplifies your power and helps you stay committed.

The Monster in the Rearview Mirror

We all make mistakes. We all wrestle with inner battles that can lead to poor decisions. But the real danger lies in letting those challenges define who we are. We start whispering things to ourselves like, "I'm just not good with money," "I'm not capable," or "I'm destined to fail."

Guess what? **Those thoughts become self-fulfilling prophecies.** The more we dwell on them, the more they sabotage our potential. Learning to control that inner narrative is crucial, but that's a story for another chapter.

When I got married at 20 and became a homeowner in the same year, I had no clue about the financial storm that was brewing. Fresh-faced and naive, I thought life would just fall into place. I grew up in a sheltered environment, and adulthood hit me hard.

I had a decent job as an administrative assistant, but things like credit, budgeting, and managing money? Complete mysteries.

Bills? *Eh, I'll pay them when I can.*

Overdrafts? *Annoying, but I'll catch up on my next paycheck.*

That ignorance was a ticking time bomb, and soon enough, the fallout began. Late fees piled up, my credit score tanked, and financial stress became my constant companion.

We weren't extravagant spenders, but my lack of financial literacy took a toll. Because I hadn't learned even the basics of managing money, we were teetering on the edge of financial ruin. But did I eventually learn to pay bills on time? Absolutely. Did I master the art of smart financial decisions? You bet I did.

What I learned along the way is this: hardships and failures aren't dead ends. They're stepping stones. They're opportunities for growth, valuable lessons wrapped in uncomfortable packaging.

We all carry the past with us—a mix of triumphs, stumbles, and regrets. But here's the kicker: if you fixate on your past mistakes, if you let those failures live rent-free in your mind (a.k.a. the monster in the rearview mirror), you can't see the road ahead. Imagine trying to drive forward while only looking in the rearview mirror. It's a dangerous game.

Instead, choose to acknowledge your past, learn from it, and then—with your eyes focused ahead and your heart determined—move forward. Your past is a chapter, not the whole story. Keep driving, but make sure you're looking through the windshield, not just the rearview mirror.

Learning from the Monster in the Rearview Mirror

How do you use the rearview mirror effectively, without letting it control your direction? Here are some key strategies:

1. **Acknowledge Your Mistakes.** Don't shy away from your past missteps. Take ownership and analyze them objectively. What went wrong? What could you have done differently?

2. **Extract the Lesson.** Look for the learning opportunity hidden within each mistake. What did you discover about yourself or the situation? How can you apply this knowledge in the future?

3. **Forgive Yourself.** Holding onto guilt and self-blame only hinders your progress. Forgive yourself for past errors and move on with a clean slate.

4. **Focus On Your Growth.** Shift your focus from dwelling on the past to actively pursuing your goals. What are you working toward? How can you use the lessons learned to make better decisions going forward?

Moving Beyond Your Past

We've all been haunted by that monster in the rearview mirror, replaying poor choices, fueling self-doubt, and letting it hold us back. But here's the truth: letting go doesn't mean forgetting. It's about acknowledging those bumps in the road, learning from them, and refusing to let them define your worth.

Think about it—the most successful people aren't those who've never fallen. They're the ones who've faced challenges, made mistakes, and used those lessons to rise stronger. It's not the regrets that push them forward—it's the growth that comes from each stumble.

If you keep looking back, it's like trying to drive while staring in your rearview mirror. You'll never reach your destination if you're not focused on what's ahead.

In the next chapter, we're going to shift gears and start envisioning your **Garden of Dreams**. We'll explore how to plant the seeds of your goals and nurture them into reality—because what lies ahead is where your true potential blooms. Let's get ready to cultivate that vision!

CHAPTER 3

CULTIVATE YOUR GARDEN
OF DREAMS

Close your eyes and take a deep, calming breath. Now imagine yourself stepping into a hidden paradise, a secret garden overflowing with life.

Sunlight filters through the trees, casting a soft glow over a vibrant tapestry of flowers in every color you can imagine. Sun-drenched roses slowly unfurl their petals, filling the air with a rich, intoxicating scent that mixes with the sweet whispers of honeysuckle.

Butterflies, like little stained-glass wonders, flutter between towering sunflowers reaching for the sky. Hummingbirds hum a gentle melody as they sip nectar from proud trumpet lilies. This garden is a symphony for your senses, a living reminder of the beauty and endless possibility surrounding you.

Now, open your eyes, and let that feeling of vibrancy and potential bloom in your heart. Because this, my friend, is more than just a garden. It's your Garden of Dreams, a breathtaking landscape waiting for your touch. Imagine yourself as the artist, not just planting seeds, but cultivating a masterpiece of your own design.

Here, the rules are yours to write. You choose the most breath-taking blooms—the goals that set your soul on fire and fuel your deepest purpose. From soaring business aspirations to nurturing your wellbeing, this garden flourishes in every facet of your life. Each blossoming bud, a testament to your vision and dedication.

In this garden, you're not at the mercy of the seasons. Here, you have the power to create the perfect environment for your dreams to thrive. Picture yourself meticulously tending each stem, providing the ideal amount of water, sunlight, and nurturing care. You become the master gardener of your own destiny, ensuring your Garden of Dreams is always in peak condition, bursting with vibrant possibilities.

Imagine the exhilarating feeling of transforming your wildest desires into a reality that explodes with color and life. That's the magic we create when we take control of our outcomes and cultivate our own Garden of Dreams.

This is a journey of self-discovery, growth, and the sweet satisfaction of witnessing your dreams blossom into something truly remarkable. Are you ready to step into your garden and paint a masterpiece with your life?

From Seed to Bloom: Cultivating Your Outcomes

Have you ever held a seed in your palm, that tiny speck holding the potential for a vibrant flower? Imagine a desired outcome (a goal you're dreaming about) as a seed—small, defined, and full of promise. But just like a seed won't blossom on its own, our outcomes need a little nurturing to truly flourish.

Every day, every hour, every action holds the potential for a harvest. Each of your desired outcomes, big or small, is an individual seed for your garden. Maybe you want to hit a revenue goal, finish a personal project, learn a new skill, or simply hold a productive meeting with your team. Perhaps it's completing a specific project for the day, like finishing a presentation or clearing your inbox. Whatever it is, it represents a clear intention, a single "thing" you want to achieve.

Now, here's the magic: that seed doesn't stay a seed forever. When planted in fertile ground, with care and attention, it begins to transform. The roots dig deep, searching for nourishment. The first delicate shoot emerges, reaching for the sunlight. Slowly but surely, the seed unfolds, revealing its true potential—a beautiful, vibrant flower.

This is the journey of a nurtured outcome. Just like we wouldn't expect a seed to instantly bloom, we shouldn't expect instant success in what we're looking to accomplish. The key is to be patient with ourselves.

We need to provide the right environment for our outcomes, goals, and dreams to take root. This means surrounding ourselves with positive influences, breaking down our outcomes into manageable steps, and feeding our motivation with knowledge and action.

As we nurture our larger outcomes (our big goals and dreams, a.k.a. big flowers), they begin to grow. We learn new things, overcome challenges, and surprise ourselves with our resilience. The journey of growth becomes a beautiful part of the process. There's a joy in watching our outcomes (flowers) take shape, even before they're fully bloomed.

The next time you're envisioning something for your future, remember the power of the seed. With dedication and care, even the smallest spark of an idea can transform into something truly awe-inspiring. Hold onto your dreams, nurture them with love and effort, and watch them blossom into the vibrant reality you deserve.

Planting the Seeds of Success: Building the Strategy

With the outcome seed in your hand, you're ready to plant it and are excited by its potential. You can almost smell the sweetness of success. But before you grab your gardening gloves and dive in, there's a crucial step: building your strategy.

Think of this strategy as the secret weapon that transforms those hopeful seeds into flourishing realities. It's about *planning before planting*, ensuring every action you take is fueled by a clear roadmap.

A Tale of Two Florists

Once upon a time, on a charming street in San Francisco, lived two passionate flower enthusiasts, Rose and Lily. Both dreamed of owning floral shops, brimming with creativity and fragrant blooms.

Rose and Lily had equal talent and the same resources at their fingertips, but their approaches were as distinct as a bold sunflower standing tall and a delicate daisy swaying in the breeze.

Rose's Petal Palace

Rose, eager to open her doors, dove headfirst into her business. Her shop overflowed with a kaleidoscope of flowers, catering to every whim. Customers browsed daily specials, from vibrant bouquets to delicate arrangements.

Rose believed hard work and staying up to date with current trends were the key to success. However, her approach was a gamble. Some days brought smiles and bustling sales while others felt stagnant.

Despite constant activity, her revenue was unstable. Her shop was popular, yet profits fluctuated, leaving Rose feeling overwhelmed and struggling for consistent growth.

Lily's Lovely Lilies

Lily, on the other hand, had a vision blooming brighter than a radiant hibiscus. She meticulously planned every aspect of her business, starting with her desired outcomes. Lily craved a thriving shop renowned for its exquisite, customized wedding bouquets.

She defined a strategy to create unique, breathtaking arrangements that captured the essence of each couple's love story.

She knew exactly what it would take to bring her stunning arrangements to life, and she identified the business skills needed to run a thriving operation and generate consistent revenue.

Lily established systems, including a personalized consultation process, a reliable supplier network, and a meticulous inventory management system (just to name a few!).

With her desired outcomes at the forefront and her strategies, skills, and systems in place, Lily built a flourishing, profitable business.

The Result

After a year, Rose's shop remained unpredictable. Her days were a rollercoaster of feast or famine. Meanwhile, Lily's shop blossomed with a loyal clientele. Her name was synonymous with stunning, personalized wedding bouquets. Her profits were consistent, and she operated with less stress and more fulfillment.

The Lesson

The tale of these two florists reveals the power of Boss^{2}ing Up. Rose, lacking a defined strategy and plan, found herself overwhelmed and stressed. Lily, however, by outlining the strategies, skills, and systems needed to bring her target outcomes to life, created a path to prosperity.

Your business, just like Lily's, has the power to flourish. With a crystal-clear vision for your goals, paired with the right strategies, skills, and systems, you'll pave your path to success. Remember, a thriving business isn't a coincidence—it's the result of a well-crafted plan, executed with precision.

Why Build the Strategy First?

Here's the scoop: by prioritizing strategy, you avoid the chaos of haphazard action. No more scrambling for what you should do next. Instead, you'll have a defined plan to keep your target outcomes (a.k.a. the seeds in your Garden of Dreams) consistently nourished and growing. We'll cover how to do that in Chapter 4!

A "Strategy-First" approach allows you to:

- **Focus Your Energy.** By planning first, you allocate your energy efficiently, knowing exactly what steps to take and when.

- **Avoid Overwhelm.** Breaking down your goals into manageable pieces prevents feeling overwhelmed by the big picture.

- **Increase Your Chances of Success.** A well-defined strategy increases your odds of achieving your goals by guiding you every step of the way.

The next time you face a goal that feels out of reach, remember this: your strategy is your greatest asset. Lay down the plan first, and then watch as your dreams unfold into vibrant, unstoppable realities.

To plot your garden of dreams in a tangible way, head over to **LiveBigWithStacey.com/resources** and download my **Strategy Planning Workbook** to start taking action on everything you're about to learn.

CHAPTER 4

IDENTIFY, CRAFT, SPRINKLE, REPEAT

Now that we've discovered the importance of building our strategy first, let's get our hands dirty and get to work.

How do we create the strategy? It all happens in three simple steps. First, identify your dream seeds. Second, craft your watering cans. And third, sprinkle with daily action. Let's look at each one in detail.

1. Identify Your Dream Seeds

First things first. What are those magnificent blooms or target outcomes (also known as your Dream Seeds) you want to see in your Garden of Dreams? Write them down. This act of putting pen to paper crystallizes your vision and makes it feel tangible.

When you're identifying your Dream Seed(s)—and, yes, you can have more than one—be laser-focused and specific. Skip vague goals like "grow my business." Instead, aim for something measurable like "increase profits by 20% this year."

Your Dream Seeds should focus solely on you and what *you* can control. For example, setting a goal like "convince my son to join my business" isn't solid because it depends on someone else buying into your vision. Keep your targets centered on your own actions and outcomes.

2. Craft Your Watering Cans

Your watering cans are the 3–4 key focus areas that will nurture each Dream Seed and help them grow.

Let's take the example of "increase profits by 20% this year." Ask yourself, "What are three to four core things I need to focus on to make that happen?" Perhaps your Watering Cans (a.k.a. key focus areas) for this Dream Seed would be:

> **Watering Can #1—Increase Revenue**
>
> **Watering Can #2—Decrease Expenses**
>
> **Watering Can #3—Streamline Operations**

After you've written down these key focus areas, go back and fill each watering can by breaking it down even further. Ask yourself, "What are the key initiatives I'd need to focus on in order to make this happen?" As an example, if I'm looking at increasing revenue in Watering Can #1, the key initiatives might be:

1. Product or service diversification
2. Pricing strategy optimization
3. Enhancing customer experience

Once you have your key initiatives written, go back and fill in 2–3 bullet points under each to give it more clarity. Keeping with the same example of increasing revenue, let's explore what that could look like, noting systems, processes, and skills needed.

Dream Seed: Increase profits by 20% this year.

Watering Can #1: Increase Revenue	System	Process	Skill
1. Product or service diversification			
a. New products/services offered to clients			
i. Market research	✓		✓
ii. Product development		✓	
iii. Project management	✓		✓
b. Expand into new markets			
i. Market analysis		✓	✓
ii. Local expertise			✓
iii. Sales & marketing communications	✓		✓
c. Bundling products and services			
i. Product management		✓	
ii. Sales & marketing communications	✓		✓
iii. Pricing strategy		✓	✓
2. Pricing strategy optimization			
a. Tiered pricing			
i. Market research		✓	✓

ii. Implementation		✓	
iii. Staff training	✓		✓
b. Discounts for bulk purchases			
i. Market research		✓	✓
ii. Implementation		✓	
iii. Supply chain management	✓		✓
c. Loyalty program to encourage repeat business			
i. Customer insights collection & data analysis	✓		✓
ii. Product development		✓	✓
iii. Marketing communications	✓	✓	✓
3. Enhancing customer experience			
a. Personalizing customer interactions			
i. Customer insights collection & data analysis	✓		✓
ii. CRM (customer relationship management software)	✓		
iii. Segmentation and targeting		✓	
b. Formalized training protocols			
i. Curriculum development		✓	✓
ii. Staff training	✓		✓

iii. Evaluation & continuous improvement	✓		✓
c. Implementing feedback systems			
i. Survey design		✓	✓
ii. Communication		✓	✓
iii. Project management	✓		✓

See how we started with a big-picture goal like increasing revenue, and now we've built a clear roadmap to make it happen? Pretty exciting, right?

Next, take each focus area and ask yourself, "Do I have the skills to do this? Is this work I'd truly enjoy? Do I have the time to dedicate to this? Do I want to own this initiative?" If the answer is yes to each of those questions, then assign yourself as the owner—the person who's going to be in the "driver's seat" of completing that item.

If the answer is no, ask yourself, "Who's my who?"—meaning, who do you have on your team (or who do you need to hire) to own that initiative and bring it to life?

Within each initiative, jot down the skills and people needed to drive the focus area forward.

Pay attention to the trends you spot. If certain skills and people are needed across multiple initiatives and you don't currently have them, those should be your hiring focus. Filling those key roles first will create the greatest impact on your business in the fastest way possible.

A Crucial Takeaway

One of the biggest pitfalls entrepreneurs face is trying to do everything themselves. Don't fall into this business-crushing trap. Delegate anything that's outside your genius zone, doesn't spark your passion, or isn't the best use of your brainpower.

Remember, you don't always need to hire employees. A coach, mentor, consultant, or freelancer could bring the expertise you need. Think outside the box!

As Gino Wickman says, "Delegate to elevate." This is the key to not only building a sustainable business but also avoiding burnout along the way.

3. Sprinkle with Daily Action

Think of your daily actions as the refreshing droplets from your Watering Can—focused tasks that fuel your growth and bring you closer to your goals. Turn each Watering Can initiative into specific, actionable steps that create a clear to-do list to keep you moving forward.

Ask yourself, "What are the things I will do this week to drive this initiative forward?" Repeat this every week until the initiative is complete.

And if you need to make a hire, those action steps could be as simple as writing a job description or sourcing candidates. These are the small, yet critical, first steps toward progress.

If someone else owns the initiative, or once you've made that key hire, hold regular check-ins to track progress, answer questions, and tackle any roadblocks. Remember, you're the leader of your business—so lead your team with confidence and clarity.

Stick to this process, and before you know it, your Garden of Dreams will start to bloom!

Example of Bringing Your Dreams to Life: A Book Blooms

Ready to watch a strategy come to life? Let's say your outcome seed is writing a book—just like this one. My outcome seed for writing *LIVE BIG* was, "Write a bestselling book in 2024."

From there, I laid out my plan:

- **Watering Can #1—Book Content.** Identify the topic, develop an outline, conduct market research, set a word count goal, and research writing tools.
  - Skills needed: writing, research, story-telling, editing, project management skills
  - People needed: trusted mentors to share ideas with and utilize as a sounding board

- **Watering Can #2—Key Milestones.** Set deadlines for finishing the manuscript and create a daily writing schedule.
  - Skills needed: project planning, time management, problem-solving, tracking & monitoring skills

- **Watering Can #3—Partners.** Identify editor, publisher, and PR partners. Define selection criteria.

- Skills needed: networking, research, communication, financial acumen, decision-making, strategic thinking
- People needed: other authors—network with them to gain referrals

Sprinkle Seeds with Action

Here are a few examples of the action steps that poured out of each of my Watering Cans:

- **Book Content**
  - Brainstorm potential book topics (Check!)
  - Research similar books in the market (Check!)
  - Create an outline for the chapters (Check!)
  - Determine any supplemental materials I might need (Check!)

- **Key Milestones**
  - Set a target date for finishing my manuscript (Check!)
  - Carve out a daily writing time slot in my schedule (Check!)
  - Set a target date for selecting my dream team partners (Check!)
  - Set a target date for my book launch (HINT: Establishing a deadline will keep you motivated!) (Check!)

- **Partners**
  - Create a list of criteria for my ideal editor, publisher, and public relations person (Check!)
  - Obtain referrals from other authors (Check!)

- ○ Research potential partners who fit the bill (Check!)
- ○ Schedule interviews with potential partners to find my perfect fit (Check!)
- ○ Sign contracts and celebrate my awesome team (Check!)

See how a seemingly daunting task like writing a book becomes manageable when you break it down like this?

When you define your target outcomes (your Dream Seeds) and build your strategy first by identifying and filling your Watering Cans, the next steps become crystal clear. This process ensures your actions are strategically aligned with your goals (Boss² Up), so every move you make helps that Dream Seed grow.

Do You Have the LIVE BIG 90-Day Momentum Maker?

As you work through this book, a blank journal will do the trick, but if you're serious about taking things to the next level, grab the **LIVE BIG 90-Day Momentum Maker**. It's the exact tool I use to turn big dreams into daily wins. This journal/planner hybrid is designed to keep you laser-focused on what truly matters.

While the daily planner will help you map out your steps, the reflective journal prompts will keep you motivated and on track, because it's not just about staying organized—it's about building momentum, celebrating progress, and unlocking your full potential every day.

Ready to stay focused and create real results? This is your roadmap to building the business and life you've been dreaming of!

**Scan the QR code or visit the link below
to grab your copy.**

LiveBigWithStacey.com/momentum

How to Weed Out Trouble and Keep Your Dreams Alive

We've talked about planting the seeds of your dreams, nurturing them with initiatives, and showering them with daily actions. But even the most vibrant garden isn't immune to pesky weeds. In our metaphorical garden, these weeds represent the problems, doubts, and negativity that can threaten to choke out your beautiful aspirations.

Just like a neglected flower bed, if left unchecked, these weeds can quickly take over. They'll steal your focus, drain your energy, and ultimately prevent your dreams from reaching their full potential.

So, how do we keep these weeds at bay? Get a trusty weeding fork and get ready to do *proactive* problem-solving.

The Art of De-Weeding

- **Regular Inspection.** Schedule regular "garden inspections." During these inspections, identify any weeds that have sprouted—negative thoughts, self-doubt, or unexpected challenges.

- **Root Cause Analysis.** Don't just pull the weed by the stem! Dig deeper and understand the root cause of the problem. Is it a lack of knowledge, a fear of failure, or an external obstacle?

- **Targeted Solutions.** Just like specific herbicides target different weeds, tailor your solutions to the specific problem. Feeling overwhelmed? Break down a large task into smaller, manageable actions. Struggling with self-doubt? Understand what's behind this limiting belief and build a plan to combat it.

Consistency is key!

Weeding isn't a one-time event. It's an ongoing process that needs to be integrated into your gardening routine. By regularly inspecting your metaphorical garden and proactively addressing problems, you ensure that your precious dreams have the space and resources to thrive.

Think of it like this: the more weeding you do, the more fertile ground there is for positivity to take root. You'll create a flourishing ecosystem where your dreams can blossom into magnificent realities.

Understanding Your Mental Soil

You've envisioned the breathtaking blooms you desire—your dreams, goals, and aspirations. You've carefully chosen the seeds you want to plant, each one representing a specific outcome you want to cultivate. You've even picked out the perfect watering cans—those crucial initiatives that will provide the essential nourishment for growth. But before we get sprinkling with daily actions, there's a fundamental element to address: the soil.

Just like in a real garden, the quality of the soil directly impacts the success of your seeds.

In your Garden of Dreams, the soil represents the fertile ground where your seeds take root. Your soil is your mindset. It's the foundation that provides the nourishment and support needed for your seeds to germinate and ultimately blossom into vibrant realities.

The right mindset cultivates a thriving garden, while a neglected one leaves seeds dormant and dreams unrealized.

Imagine planting a rosebush in pure sand. The sun might be perfect, the watering meticulous, but the rosebush will still struggle. The sand lacks the nutrients and structure needed for growth.

Similarly, our mental soil can be a rich loam, teeming with optimism and resilience, or it can be a dense clay, heavy with negativity and self-doubt.

The Different Types of Mental Soil

Just like physical soil has various compositions, our mental soil comes in different forms. Let's explore some common types:

- **Sandy Soil.** This mind struggles with focus and commitment. Ideas flow freely, but sticking to a plan proves challenging. The good news is that sandy soil is easily amended with routines and goal-setting exercises.

- **Clay Soil.** Here, negativity and self-doubt run rampant. Overthinking and pessimism can suffocate dreams before they even start to sprout. Mindfulness practices and positive affirmations can help break through this mental barrier.

- **Silty Soil.** This fertile ground is receptive to ideas but lacks structure. Enthusiasm is high, but organization and planning might need work. Implementing project management tools and setting milestones can help transform this soil into a powerhouse.

- **Loamy Soil.** Ah, the gardener's dream! This balanced mind is a blend of optimism, focus, and resilience. It readily absorbs new information and thrives on challenges. However, even the best soil can become depleted, so ongoing self-care and positive reinforcement are key.

Enriching Your Mental Soil: Cultivating a Fertile Landscape for Growth

Unlike physical soil, our mental soil is remarkably dynamic. We can actively improve its quality through various practices, which we'll walk through later in this book. In fact, you can even change your soil type altogether—so, whether you have sandy, clay, or silty soil today, you can actually swap your soil for that rich, lush, loamy soil through practices like:

- **Positive Affirmations.** Regularly repeating empowering statements can combat negativity and boost confidence.

- **Visualizations.** Vividly picturing success scenarios can prime your mind for actual achievement.

- **Gratitude Practice.** Focusing on what you're grateful for fosters a positive outlook and fuels motivation.

- **Self-Compassion.** Acknowledging and learning from setbacks without dwelling on them promotes emotional well-being.

- **Learning and Growth.** Continuously seeking knowledge and new skills keeps your mind sharp and adaptable.

By nurturing your mental soil, you create the perfect environment for your dreams to come alive.

The Dream Gardener's Toolkit

You're nurturing your soil (mindset), and you've chosen the perfect Watering Cans (focus areas) to help your Dream Seeds (target outcomes) flourish; you're sprinkling your seeds with daily action and have learned to identify and banish those pesky weeds (problems). That's fantastic!

But just like a real garden bursting with life, your dream oasis needs a dedicated care routine to stay vibrant.

Here's where things really get exciting. What I'm about to share with you is like your personal gardening guide, a three-tiered approach to keeping your Garden of Dreams thriving.

Consider it as a schedule of check-ins that ensure your dreams blossom into beautiful realities—I call it the "Dream Gardener's Toolkit," and here's how it works ...

Monthly Review: Strategic Pruning

Imagine your monthly review as a strategic pruning session. Grab your metaphorical pruning shears, set a timer for 60 minutes, and focus on the bigger picture:

- **Growth Assessment.** How are your seeds progressing? Have some initiatives yielded significant progress? Are any seeds struggling to germinate?

- **Refinement.** Have your circumstances or priorities shifted? It's okay to refine the key focus areas in your Watering Cans based on new information.

- **Course Correction.** Did you encounter unexpected challenges? This is the time to identify any major weeds (problems) and develop strategies to address them.

- **Nourishment Planning.** Evaluate your current "soil" (mindset). Are there any areas needing improvement, like boosting your confidence or managing stress? Schedule activities to nurture your mental well-being.

Weekly Check-In: Weed Patrol and Progress Tracking

Think of your weekly check-in as a 30-minute weed patrol and progress-tracking session:

- **Weed Patrol.** Inspect your garden for any new weeds sprouting—negative thoughts, self-doubt, or roadblocks. Nip them in the bud with proactive problem-solving.

- **Action Review.** Review your daily actions for the past week. Did they effectively nurture your seeds?

- **Initiative Check.** Are you on track to achieve the initiatives that are inside your Watering Cans? Adjust your approach if needed.

- **Celebrate Success.** Acknowledge and celebrate your wins, no matter how small. This reinforces your progress and keeps you motivated.

Daily Huddle: Seed Sprinkling & Hydration

Your daily huddle is a 15-minute self check-in and your chance to give your seeds a vital sprinkle:

- **Action Planning.** Review your actions for the day. These are the small, focused tasks that stem from your initiatives.

- **Mindset Boost.** Start your day with a positive affirmation or visualization exercise to nourish your "mental soil" and maintain a growth-oriented attitude.

- **Limit Lifting.** Identify any lingering doubts or challenges and devise a plan to tackle them.

We've spent some beautiful time cultivating our Garden of Dreams, planting the Dream Seeds of our wildest aspirations. But a thriving garden doesn't just happen by chance. It requires intention, care, and the right tools. If you're like me, having a visual reminder can make all the difference. That's where the **Dream Gardener's Toolkit** comes in.

Head over to **LiveBigWithStacey.com/resources**, grab your copy, print it out, and put it in a frame. Keep it on your desk as a constant reminder of your dreams and the steps to bring them to life!

In the next chapter, we'll explore how to truly "show up" for yourself, transforming your dreams from vibrant possibilities into a flourishing reality. Get ready to discover the secrets to becoming the master gardener of your own life, where intentionality becomes the fertile ground in which your dreams take root and blossom.

Pay It Forward | Leave a Review and Empower a Fellow Entrepreneur

If you're finding value in this book so far, I have a simple request that could make a massive impact. By taking 60 seconds to leave a review, you're not just sharing your thoughts—you're paying it forward.

Your review could help another female entrepreneur discover the tools and insights that could change her life, just like you're doing right now. Best of all, it's completely free!

Leaving a review online is easy:

1. Head over to the page where you purchased the book.
2. Scroll down to the section that says "Customer Reviews" and click "Write a customer review."
3. Share your honest feedback and hit submit.

Thank you for being part of this journey with me. Your voice matters more than you know!

CHAPTER 5

LEARN THE LANGUAGE
OF YOUR GODROD

As a teenager, my musical obsession wasn't exactly mainstream. While my friends were blasting pop icons like Whitney and Madonna, I was filling my ears with the rich harmonies of barbershop quartets like the one my dad sang in when I was a child.

I'm totally dating myself here, but back then, record players and cassette tapes (not fancy streaming services) ruled the audio world. Every night, I'd pull out my favorite barbershop quartet cassette tape, slip it into my trusty gray boombox, and let the beautiful harmonies lull me to sleep. It was the perfect soundtrack for my teenage dreams.

In 1991, the international barbershop convention was being held in Louisville, just an hour away from my home in Columbus, Indiana. I'd been attending regional barbershop events with my parents for years, but this was the big leagues!

We arrived Wednesday evening and headed straight to the headquarters hotel for registration. The moment I stepped into that lobby and saw all my musical heroes in person, it felt like stepping into a fantasy land. The energy in the air was electric, and "tag

singing" (a beloved tradition) was happening in every corner—
and the lobby was chock-full of cute guys to meet, an important
priority for my 16-year-old self. The next four days were simply
electrifying, and I left that convention feeling "hooked on barbershop" like never before.

The following year, the convention was in New Orleans, and I des-
perately wanted to experience all the magic again. Thankfully, I
managed to convince my parents to take me as my high school
graduation gift. So, in the summer of 1992, we piled into our
trusty beige van and embarked on a trip to the "Big Easy."

The convention was everything I'd hoped for: reconnecting with
my musical idols, immersing myself in the music I loved, and, you
guessed it, meeting boys! Then, on July 3rd, 1992, at the sprightly
age of 17, I met Chad. He wasn't just a cute guy—he was different,
something I couldn't quite put my finger on.

That first night we met, we spent hours singing, laughing, and
talking. We met up the following evening to continue talking,
and before we knew it, we were lost in conversation until the early
hours of the morning.

my brother, Gary, was supposed to be my chaperone, but Chad and
I were having so much fun that I convinced Gary to head back to
our hotel without me, leaving me at the headquarters hotel alone.
(Of course, my parents were less than thrilled when they found out
my brother left me alone in one of the most dangerous cities in the
U.S.) But Chad made sure I got back safely—he called a cab, rode
with me, and saw to it that I made it to my hotel without a scratch.

The following day, my parents packed up our brown van, and we
headed for home. During the 12-hour ride back to Indiana, I found

myself replaying the incredible memories of the week, especially those involving Chad. I couldn't seem to stop thinking about him.

That next weekend, Chad made the drive from Ohio to Indiana to visit me, and as soon as he headed home, I found myself, once again, unable to stop thinking about him. There was an undeniable pull, something I couldn't quite explain. It was the first time I truly experienced a gut feeling, a deep knowing unlike anything I'd encountered before. This feeling of certainty would later become a cornerstone of my personal and professional growth.

Years later, I've come to understand the immense power of intuition, something we all possess. That unexplainable inner voice, that quiet nudge that steers us in the right direction. For me, this intuition is more than just a feeling. It's a guiding force, a connection to something bigger than myself.

I call it my "GodRod."

Imagine a steel rebar, strong and unwavering, stabilized through the very core of your being. This isn't a flimsy antenna you can attach or detach at will. It's anchored deep within you, its roots intertwined with your values, beliefs, and your faith. This rebar extends upward, and emerges proudly at the crown of your head, acting as your personal GPS. This is your GodRod.

Just like rebar strengthens concrete, your GodRod provides an inner strength and support system. It allows you to face challenging decisions with unwavering confidence, guiding you toward opportunities and connections that logic alone might miss.

Now, let's wrap up my story with Chad. Even though I couldn't explain it at the time, I knew, clear as day, he was *the one*. I followed my intuition, and it led me right. Now, at the time of this writing, Chad and I have just celebrated our 30th wedding anniversary, and I'm grateful every day that, at just 17, I listened to my inner voice.

While my faith informs my personal view of intuition, I understand that this concept has many interpretations. Call it your GodRod, your intuition, or just a gut feeling—the key takeaway is to recognize its power and learn to leverage it effectively.

Here's why trusting your GodRod is the ultimate LIVE BIG move:

- **Decisions on Fire.** Sometimes, you gotta make a call, fast! That's when your GodRod swoops in like a superhero. It combines your past experiences, sneaky subconscious wisdom, and pure intuition to give you instant insights. It's like having a secret advisor whispering the best choice in your ear. Plus, it goes beyond logic, leading you to well-rounded decisions that feel just right.

- **Aligned and Authentic You.** Ever feel like a fake because your head says one thing and your heart says another? Trusting your GodRod keeps you true to yourself and your business vision. It helps you make choices that resonate with your core values, building a sense of integrity that shines through to your team, clients, and everyone you meet. Talk about Boss²ing Up!

- **Ultimate Radar.** Analysis paralysis is no fun! While data and logic are important, sometimes they can leave you spinning. Your GodRod cuts through the noise, giving you the confidence to make quick decisions, especially when time is tight. It's like having a built-in, high-powered radar that helps you navigate tricky situations.

- **Opportunity Spotter.** The world is full of hidden gems, and your GodRod is strategically navigating a treasure map behind the scenes. It helps you sniff out amazing opportunities that might go unnoticed otherwise. Trust your instincts and go explore those innovative ideas. You never know what you might find!

- **Risk Whisperer.** Your GodRod is like your own personal danger alarm. It sends subtle signals—a flicker of unease or a "feeling" in the pit of your stomach—to warn you of potential risks or situations that just don't feel right. By listening to these gut feelings, you can make informed decisions to avoid pitfalls and potentially harmful situations.

- **Thinking Outside the Box.** Logic is great, but sometimes you gotta break the mold! Your GodRod can help you think non-linearly, opening doors to creative solutions and unconventional approaches. It's like having a built-in brainstorming buddy, always ready to help you solve problems in a whole new way.

- **Building Bridges.** Trusting your GodRod fosters authenticity, and that's magnetic! It shows confidence and conviction in your decisions, which goes a long way in building strong relationships with your clients, partners, and team members. People appreciate a leader who follows their instincts!

- **EQ Master.** Your GodRod and emotional intelligence are best friends. By trusting your intuition, you become a master at understanding others, making better judgments, and building a team that truly clicks.

Your GodRod is a secret weapon for making incredible decisions, seizing opportunities, and building a business that's true to you.

Intuition Unleashed: How to Tap Into Your Own GodRod

Ready to turn that inner murmur into a game-changing super-power? Let's dive into a step-by-step plan to tap into your GodRod, so you can become the ultimate decision-making machine.

Step 1: Silence the Chatter

Think of your intuition like a shy friend at a crowded party. All the noise drowns them out! To hear your GodRod clearly, you have to create some quiet space. Dedicate time each day to meditation, journaling, or simply taking a nature walk. Let the mental chatter settle, and open yourself to the subtle whispers of your inner voice.

These days, I dedicate more than a few minutes each day for self-exploration. Sometimes it's an entire weekend! Regardless of how long you spend, it's incredibly important to just give yourself "space for space," as one of my mentors calls it. Spending time with silence around you opens your ears so you can begin to hear what your intuition is telling you.

Step 2: Get Body Smart

You're hustling at a networking event, the air buzzing with ideas and possibilities. You strike up a conversation with a fellow entrepreneur and their business concept sounds intriguing. You discuss part-nering together, which could be a game changer for your business.

Days later, they send a collaboration proposal that includes a 50/50 revenue share, and while the financial split seems fair, a flicker of unease sparks in your gut. Something feels off. This, my friend, is your GodRod—your intuition—whispering a warning. Pay attention to it.

Your GodRod isn't a booming voice from the heavens, it's a subtle symphony playing within you. Sometimes it's a flutter of your heart, a surge of excitement. Other times, it's an uncomfortable feeling in the pit in your stomach. My GodRod often will put a "heavy" feeling on my chest if something is off.

These physical cues are your GodRod's way of giving you the inside scoop.

Think of it like this: you wouldn't ignore a flashing red light on your car's dashboard, would you? That light is a warning, a signal to take action. Your GodRod operates in a similar way.

A sudden wave of nausea before a big presentation? Your intuition might be sensing some last-minute details you haven't considered.

A tightness in your jaw while talking to a potential business partner? Your GodRod might be picking up on a mismatch in values.

The key is to learn the language of your GodRod. Pay attention to the subtle shifts in your body—the goosebumps, the chills, the butterflies. These are all whispers of wisdom waiting to be heard. The more you tune in, the clearer the messages become.

Here's the best part: your GodRod isn't just about avoiding danger zones. It's your personal compass, leading you toward opportunities and experiences that align with your deepest desires.

That feeling of pure joy when you stumble upon a hidden gem of a coffee shop? Your GodRod might be nudging you toward a space that sparks creativity or a chance encounter with someone special.

The next time you feel that tug in your gut or a bounce in your step, don't brush it off. Trust your intuition, lean into it, and watch as your life unfolds with more meaning and alignment than ever before. Your GodRod is always there, guiding you toward your best self.

And hey, I get it—this might sound a little "woo-woo." But here's the thing: the more you tune into your GodRod, even if it feels strange at first, the stronger and more confident you'll become in making decisions that truly serve you. Embrace it because that inner voice is your greatest ally.

Step 3: Practice Makes Progress

Tapping into your intuition is like strengthening a muscle. It requires practice, patience, and trust. Start with something small. Maybe it's choosing a restaurant based on a gut feeling, or trying a new method for a task simply because it feels right. Do it again with another small decision, and again. With each step, you'll build the confidence to trust your inner compass more deeply.

When it comes to bigger decisions, your GodRod is your powerful ally. Yes, data and logic are essential, but don't forget to "check in" with your intuition. Sometimes, there's a pull you can't fully explain, a feeling that defies logic but simply feels *right*. Don't ignore that.

Every time you weigh your decisions against your GodRod, you're reinforcing your confidence in your own judgment, aligning yourself with a deeper truth that will guide you in the right direction. Trust it—it's there to serve you.

Step 4: Celebrate the Wins (and Learn from the Losses)

Your entrepreneurial journey will be filled with both triumphs and setbacks. The important part is celebrating the wins *and* learning from the losses, all while recognizing how your GodRod played a role in each.

Recently, I hosted a retreat, and let's be real—it was no small commitment. It came with a hefty price tag and happened right when many kids were going back to school. Several of the women who attended felt like they just didn't have the time. Some missed their kids' first day back, and one incredible woman even missed her son's first birthday. But despite all of that, they each felt a powerful, undeniable pull saying, "I need to be there." They didn't know it then, but that was their GodRod guiding them.

One attendee, a highly successful CEO with a jam-packed calendar, hesitantly committed. Even though the retreat was four days, she only carved out three, originally booking her flight to head home early. But after just the first day, she said, "What I've learned today has been life-changing. I can't leave early. I have to stay." That was her GodRod in action, leading her exactly where she needed to be.

Here's the thing—often, we don't recognize that inner knowing right away. But when we tap into it, when we listen to that gut feeling—our GodRod—it guides us toward what's right, even if it defies logic.

Sometimes that unexplainable "pull" can't be rationalized, and that's okay. Don't resist it. Trust it. Celebrate yourself for being in tune with your intuition and making decisions that align with your core. That's where the magic happens.

But what about when things don't go according to plan? Maybe you ignored that nagging voice in the back of your mind, and later realized it was spot on. Or perhaps you rushed into a decision without checking in with your gut first. Guess what? That's okay!

When you LIVE BIG, every setback becomes a learning opportunity. Instead of dwelling on what went wrong, reflect on what your intuition was trying to tell you.

What signals did you overlook? Take some time to jot down a few mental notes (or even better, talk it out with a trusted advisor) about how you can use that experience to fine-tune your decision-making moving forward.

Every lesson is a chance to grow, and when you embrace that, you'll find that even the missteps lead you closer to where you're meant to be.

Think of it like this: every success and every stumble is a piece of the puzzle. By recognizing the role your intuition played (or perhaps didn't play) in each situation, you're building a powerful map for navigating your success journey—in your business and in your life.

The next time you make a decision, big or small, take a moment to listen to that inner voice. Celebrate your wins and be proud of your progress while using your losses as stepping stones to greater wisdom. Your GodRod is always there, cheering you on, and with a little practice, you'll become a master decoder of its messages.

Step 5: Journal Your Journey

Let's face it, your GodRod isn't going to show up with a loud voice or a flashing neon sign. Instead, it speaks in whispers—and sometimes it's a simple feeling inside.

Here's where your trusty journal comes in. Your journal is your personal GodRod translator. Keep it by your side, always ready to capture these precious whispers. Don't worry about perfect grammar or lengthy entries. Jot down random thoughts that pop into your head, even if they seem outlandish.

Did you have a vivid dream about a new product design? Scribble it down! Feeling a tightness in your chest while negotiating a contract term? Note it! There are no wrong answers when it comes to deciphering your GodRod's language.

Think of your journal as a treasure map, slowly revealing the secret code of your intuition. As you consistently capture these fleeting messages, patterns may emerge. You might start to notice that a surge of butterflies in your stomach consistently precedes a brilliant business idea. Or perhaps a knot in your gut always appears when you're on the wrong track. The more you tune in and record these subtle cues, the clearer your GodRod's voice becomes.

Grab your pen and get ready to have a conversation with your wise inner guide. You might be surprised by the profound wisdom your GodRod has been whispering all along.

Your GodRod Is Your Secret Weapon, Not a Magic 8-Ball

Intuition is a powerful force, but it thrives with a partner—cold, hard logic. Don't ditch research, data, and analysis just because your gut whispers a certain direction.

Your GodRod is your compass, guiding you toward the best path. But logic and analysis are the mortar that holds everything together.

With practice, you'll learn to wield your GodRod with confidence, make decisions that are both bold and well-informed, and ultimately build a business and a life that reflects your deepest desires and values.

If you want a little help tapping into your GodRod and letting divine intuition guide your journey, don't forget to grab a copy of the **LIVE BIG 90-Day Momentum Maker**—designed to help you turn those inspired insights into purposeful action every day!

**Visit LiveBigWithStacey.com/momentum
or scan the QR code to grab your copy.**

CHAPTER 6

YOUR ENERGY ARMOR AND INNER CIRCLE

You're probably wearing what feels like a million hats and juggling a to-do list the size of Texas. How do you stay laser-focused when there's so much to tackle? Let's dive into some power moves to conquer your time, work smarter, and cultivate your Garden of Dreams.

Delegate to Elevate

"Delegate to elevate" is a powerful mantra I learned from Gino Wickman, the brilliant mind behind best-selling books like *Traction* and *Rocket Fuel*. The idea is simple: we all have 24 hours in a day, but let's be real—some days, it feels like we need a time machine just to fit everything in. That's where delegation and outsourcing become your secret weapons to reclaim your time, energy, and sanity!

Take Beyoncé, for example—she's one of the greatest performers on the planet, but do you think she does it all alone? Absolutely not. For every performance, she relies on an entire team of dancers, stylists, backup singers, and producers all working together to create the magic you see on stage.

Now, think of your business as your own personal stage. You're the star, but you don't have to be a one-woman show. By building a team and delegating tasks that don't require *your* magic touch, you free yourself up to focus on what you do best—leading, creating, and delivering on your vision. Step into that spotlight and let others help you shine!

Remember, by delegating and outsourcing, you're not giving up control, you're actually *taking* control. You're creating a powerful team, freeing yourself to focus on what truly matters—growing your Dream Seeds.

Create a Distraction-Free Zone

Create a quiet workspace that's free of clutter. Your brain will thank you! Silence those pesky phone notifications, close unnecessary browser tabs, and consider website blockers—anything to keep your focus laser-sharp. Imagine your workspace as your mission control center—clear, calm, and ready for takeoff!

Strategically Plan Your Day

You've already unlocked the power of strategic planning, and when you bring intention into every day, your focus explodes and productivity soars. The key is to start your morning with a plan, setting the tone for the day ahead. Some people swear by planning the night before, but let's be honest—by the end of the day, my brain is usually mush. So, I prefer to plan in the morning when my energy is fresh. Here's the thing: do what works best for *you*.

Here's my simple, 15-minute planning routine to kick-start each day:

1. **Start With Gratitude.**

   Begin your day by writing down three things (or people) you're grateful for and why. This small act of appreciation shifts your mindset and reshapes your outlook. You'll begin to see opportunities instead of obstacles.

2. **Set Your Three Non-Negotiables.**

   Identify the three must-do's for the day that will move your business forward and block time for them on your calendar. Yes, your to-do list may have more than three tasks, but these are non-negotiables—you're not going to bed until they're done. Everything else? Delegate where possible.

3. **Prioritize Learning.**

   Commit to feeding your brain with education daily. Whether it's 15 minutes of an audiobook or podcast while doing your makeup, or 20 minutes of reading before diving into emails—intentionally prioritize continuous learning. Your business and bank account will thank you for it!

4. **Show Up for Someone Else.**

   Think about how you can serve someone today. Maybe it's a quick text to check in on a friend or responding to a question on social media. It doesn't have to be time-consuming, but intentionally showing up for others will fill your cup.

5. **Show Up for Yourself.**

   Don't forget *you*. Write down how you're going to prioritize yourself today—whether it's hitting the gym, meditating, or enjoying a quiet coffee. Remember, you can't pour from an empty cup, so make sure you're taking care of your own well-being too.

6. **Visualize Your Success.**

Take a moment to visualize your day unfolding smoothly. See yourself solving challenges with ease and achieving your goals. This small practice can make a huge difference—whether you're picturing big dreams or mastering daily tasks, visualizing success sets you up to win.

7. **Write and Speak Your Affirmations.**

Finally, write and say your affirmations out loud. Don't skip this! Speaking them not only trains your brain for success but also reinforces your intentions for the day ahead.

By committing just 15 minutes to this morning routine, you'll bring laser focus and structure into your day. It's not just about planning—it's about building the strength to conquer challenges, show up powerfully, and ultimately, double your productivity.

Ditch Multitasking

Contrary to popular belief, multitasking actually hurts your focus and productivity. Focus on one task at a time and give it your full attention. This allows you to work smarter, not harder, and produce the top-notch results you're looking for.

Take Regular Breaks

Taking regular breaks is a powerful way to keep your mind fresh. Schedule quick 10-minute "breathers" throughout your day to recharge and refresh your mind. Stretch, take a walk, do anything that helps you relax and come back feeling rejuvenated. A happy brain is a focused brain!

Limit Social Media

Make the decision to resist distractions and stay committed to your plan for the day. This means setting boundaries around your social media use during work hours. Let's be honest—those endless scrolls on Instagram or TikTok can quickly eat away your time and energy. Try setting specific times to check in or use an app to limit your screen time.

By intentionally stepping back from social media while you're focused on work, you'll find you have more mental clarity and productivity throughout the day. Remember, social media will still be there when you're done crushing your goals—so give yourself permission to stay focused, get the work done, and reward yourself with a little scroll time later!

Get an Accountability Partner

Accountability is a secret weapon for success. When you share your goals and progress with a trusted friend, mentor, or colleague, you're not just keeping yourself on track—you're inviting in a powerful support system.

These people become your cheerleaders, your sounding boards, and your accountability partners all rolled into one. They'll celebrate your wins, push you when you need it, and help you stay focused on what matters most.

Surround yourself with people who want to see you win and watch how much faster you reach your goals when you've got someone in your corner holding you accountable.

Staying focused in a world full of distractions isn't always easy. Be patient with yourself, celebrate your progress, and remember, you've got the tools and the power to achieve anything you set your mind to.

The Art of Being Intentional

Accidents are an inevitable part of our lives. You accidentally send an email to the wrong person. Or accidentally put your coffee creamer away in the cabinet instead of in the fridge (yep, I just did that last week). You accidentally butt-dial someone—even worse, now with technology advancements, you can accidentally butt FaceTime someone. (Just did that recently, too!)

Mistakes happen. They're unavoidable, and one of the first things we do when we make a mistake is to say, "Oh, sorry, I didn't intend to do that." Then, you become more aware and focused—and you pay more attention to what you're doing. You avoid making the same mistakes by being intentional about not repeating them.

But what if you applied intention to your mindset? What would life look like for you?

I was first introduced to the concept of being intentional about your mindset by James Wedmore, and the power of this concept became crystal clear to me during a morning walk.

You see, when I visit my vacation rentals in Myrtle Beach, I often like to take power walks on the beach in the morning. After my morning coffee, I lace up my black Nikes and head out to the sand. I walk briskly for two miles, taking in the beautiful sights around me while listening to a podcast episode.

One fateful morning, I put on my headphones and tuned into James Wedmore's *Mind Your Business* podcast (one of my faves), and I stumbled upon an episode featuring John Assaraf, often referred to as "The Brain Whisperer." I was completely blown away by what I was hearing. He was talking about how our brains are the world's most powerful computers—and that we can actually program them. *Say what? Program our brains?*

Back then, I'd heard the saying "thoughts become things," but I wasn't really sure what it meant. It wasn't until John spoke about the brain being like a computer that a lightbulb truly went on for me. He talked about the fact that if you want different outputs from your computer (your brain), you have to feed it different inputs—just like programming a PC.

That simple analogy resonated deeply, and I felt like it was a key unlocking a hidden door within me.

Two days later, on my ten-hour road trip back to Ohio, I decided to explore this concept further. I pulled out my trusty travel sidekick, the Audible app, and dove straight into John Assaraf's book, *Innercise: The New Science to Unlock Your Brain's Hidden Power*. Those ten hours on the road flew by as I devoured his teachings. It was there, in the driver's seat of my black Honda Accord, that I truly discovered the incredible power within myself.

I discovered the power to rewire my brain and create the exact life I desired.

This wasn't just some abstract theory anymore. It felt real, tangible, and empowering. The potential for change was exhilarating, and I couldn't wait to start putting it into practice.

I decided to become *intentional* about my mindset and what I fed my brain on a daily basis. Fueled by this newfound excitement, "brain training" became part of my daily ritual. (I'll share some of my favorite brain exercises in just a bit.)

Now, I know the concept of daily brain exercises sounds a bit "out there" at first, but honestly, I was okay with a little "woo-woo" if these brain exercises meant unlocking my full potential. And unlock it they did.

Back then, I was stuck in a corporate job, yearning for freedom from my W2. I'd been investing in real estate on the side and had just purchased my first two short-term rentals at the beach. But my real estate portfolio wasn't generating anywhere near my six-figure salary. I was trapped by those golden handcuffs, frustrated and desperate for a new life. Every morning, I'd wake up with this heavy weight on my chest, dreaming about doing work that fulfilled me.

But the loop I was repeating in my mind? "Stacey, you make too much money to change what you're doing. *You don't want to start over.* Feeling fulfilled isn't really **that** important. You're fine. *Just deal with it.*" My brain, it seemed, was working against me.

But when I started doing daily brain exercises, I knew I was chipping away at those old patterns, rewiring my thinking for possibility. I didn't have everything figured out for my future, but I felt different. I knew I was making progress.

Every morning, as I was meditating and doing my brain exercises, I felt like a step closer to breaking free. The frustration, self-doubt, and limiting beliefs that had plagued me began to fade, replaced by a growing sense of control and optimism. I still didn't have all the answers, but I finally felt empowered to find them. And that, in itself, was a game-changer.

Fast forward to today, as I'm writing this book—it's been two years since I walked away from that corporate gig, and I've never looked back. Since then, I've made it a priority to continue my brain exercises and to be incredibly intentional about my mindset.

What I've come to realize, though, is that while I can control my own mindset, I can't control the thoughts or words of others. That's when I became intentional about the energy I allow into my life and the people I surround myself with.

Introducing Your Energy Armor

As I dove deeper into understanding the power of my mind and manifesting what I wanted in life, I discovered something incredible—the unmistakable power of positivity. But let's be real, not everyone's ready to hop on the positivity train. In fact, some people thought I was completely "coo-coo for Cocoa Puffs" for choosing to stay positive, no matter what.

One conversation sticks with me. Someone, dripping with sarcasm and mocking me in a whiny voice, said, "Stacey, you just want everything to be sunshine and rainbows, huh? Positive, positive, positive. Well, newsflash—that's not how life works!"

Here's the deal: choosing positivity doesn't mean you're living in a fantasy world. Life still throws curveballs.

Do I face tough situations? Absolutely. Do I have difficult conversations? You bet. Does shit still happen? Of course.

But here's what I've learned: I choose to respond with positivity, no matter what. Negativity is like a virus—it spreads fast, and I'm not interested in catching it. And you shouldn't be either.

Let me introduce you to a powerful mental tool: your **Energy Armor**. Picture a clear, bulletproof plexiglass box surrounding you.

Your Energy Armor serves two powerful purposes. First, it keeps your positive energy close to you, like soaking in a warm bubble bath that never loses its bubbles. That energy doesn't just fizzle away—it sticks with you throughout the day, surrounding you in positivity. And because this armor is clear, your good vibes radiate outward, positively impacting everyone around you.

But that's not all. Your Energy Armor is also an impenetrable shield against negativity. Those "energy vampires" who try to drain you? They bounce right off. No matter the situation, the negative words thrown your way, or the toxic energy brewing around you, your Energy Armor deflects it all, keeping negativity from ever penetrating your space. You're in control, and your energy stays protected and strong.

Upgrade Your Inner Circle: Surround Yourself with Those Who Fuel Your Dreams

Positivity is like a contagious superpower, but negativity is more of a buzzkill. We all have those friends or family members who, unintentionally or not, can leave us feeling drained and questioning our dreams. You are the DJ of your own vibe, and you get to choose the frequency you tune into.

Think of Jim Rohn's wisdom: "You are the average of the five people you spend the most time with." If your inner circle is filled with naysayers, it might be time for a friendly reshuffle. Surround yourself with people who fuel your fire instead of dampening it. Your inner circle should be cheerleaders—not energy vampires.

Now, sometimes distancing yourself from negative people isn't always an option, especially when they're family. But that doesn't mean you have to absorb their negativity. Here's where your Energy Armor comes in!

Remember, your Energy Armor not only radiates your positive energy outward, but it also acts as a powerful shield. No matter how fast or furious those arrows of negativity come flying at you, they bounce right off without leaving a mark. You stay protected, and your energy stays intact.

You are in control. Choose to surround yourself with positivity and use your Energy Armor to protect yourself from anything that tries to dim your light. You've got this!

A Note About Sharing Your Dreams

Picture your support system as a life cocktail—a delicious blend of friends, family, mentors, and peers, each adding their own unique flavor to your journey. The foundation of this mix? Your family and friends, who are your essential ingredients. Their unwavering belief in you and your dreams is like a potent catalyst, sparking your resilience and pushing you forward.

For me, my journey wouldn't be the same without my amazing husband, Chad (or, as I lovingly call him, "my Chadder"). He's always been my biggest supporter, and as we've grown and evolved together, so has our relationship. That's one of the most beautiful things about life, right? A key ingredient in our 30-year marriage has been open communication. Sharing your dreams with your significant other and having their support is incredibly important.

Now, I realize you may not have that built-in cheerleader at home. But here's the truth: *your dreams are valid—no exceptions.* Don't ever let anyone tell you otherwise.

If you find yourself in a situation where your spouse or partner isn't supporting you, it might be time to have a serious conversation or seek professional guidance. Also, consider surrounding yourself with other women who've successfully navigated these tricky waters.

The world is overflowing with alternative support streams waiting to be tapped into. Consider getting a mentor, joining a mastermind program, or seeking out communities where you can connect with like-minded women who "get you."

Surrounding yourself with supportive people is a powerful tool that can help you on your journey to turning your dreams into reality. Go on, mix up your own perfect life cocktail and get ready to conquer the world!

CHAPTER 7

LIVE BIG NON-NEGOTIABLES

Have you ever watched a woman glide in 4.5-inch stilettos and thought, "Wow, walking in those looks so easy!" Yeah, me neither! Walking in stilettos is an art form. It tests your strength, your balance, and your determination. But finding the perfect pair to complete a killer outfit? So worth it. Let me tell you a quick story …

Pushing Through the Fear Zone

A while back, my quartet was gearing up for a big singing competition, and we had this fierce, head-turning costume lined up—candy apple red tops that fit like a dream, paired with sleek, leather-look leggings. It was a mix of sass and class. But we were missing one thing. Shoes. We decided to each wear our own red heels, but they had to sparkle and match that perfect shade of red.

After what felt like hours of searching online, I found the shoe. It had everything—an eye-catching band of rhinestones that practically screamed, "Look at me!" It was the exact red I'd been searching for. But the heel? 4.5 inches tall. I've worn plenty of heels in my life, but nothing that high.

I thought, "Maybe I should keep looking," but no other shoe even came close. This was the one. There was just one problem—I had no idea how I was going to walk in them. Naturally, I ordered them anyway.

When the shoes arrived, it felt like my fashion fairy godmother had sprinkled magic dust all over the room. They were stunning—sassy, classy, and sky-high! I slipped them on and instantly thought, "Oh no, there's no way I can walk on stage in these, let alone stand and sing!" Walking in them had me wobbling like Bambi on ice—totally unsteady and out of my element. My first instinct was, "I've got to send these back."

But something inside me said, "Try again." So I did.

The next day, I strapped those red stilettos back on, but I still caught myself thinking, "One wrong step and I'm going down." I was convinced I needed a different pair—there was no way I could risk falling on stage. But that little voice inside whispered, "Stacey, these are the shoes. Keep going."

So, I kept practicing. I walked around the house in them, and slowly but surely, it started to click. The wobble disappeared, and after a few weeks, I could finally walk and look straight ahead instead of staring at the floor to avoid tripping. *Score!*

Then came the real test: standing and singing in them. Oh boy, was that rough. I was focused on how to not tip over rather than being focused on my singing. I sounded pretty awful. But I kept at it, practicing over and over until I could finally stand tall, walk confidently, and sing my heart out in those heels.

Conquering those stilettos became so much more than just learning to walk in uncomfortable shoes. Through that performance mastery, I discovered an inner strength and tenacity that had been lying dormant. Those red stilettos woke up a part of me that was ready to push past my fears and stay outside of my comfort zone, even when everything inside me wanted to quit.

There was a voice in my head telling me to give up, to take the easy way out, but I knew better. I knew I had to keep going, ignore those self-doubts, and push through what I call the "Fear Zone." It's that uncomfortable space where everything feels shaky, where fear and uncertainty try to hold you back. But the magic happens when you keep moving forward through it.

Here's the thing, my friend: it's not about the shoes. It's about *you.* It's about the power you unlock when you step outside your comfort zone and break through the fear. On the other side of that fear zone is where your inner peace and strength wake up, and where real growth begins.

So, how do we push through the Fear Zone?

1. Commit to it.
2. Be the person who pushes through fear (yes, you can fake it 'til you make it).
3. Do the things a courageous person does.

Commit. Be. Do.

Practice, Refine, Practice Some More

While the Commit-Be-Do approach is surprisingly simple, it requires **practice**. Malcolm Gladwell, in his book *Outliers,* argues that mastering a skill takes 10,000 hours of practice. While that might sound daunting, Josh Kaufman, author of *The Personal*

MBA, offers a more attainable approach. According to Kaufman, you can go from novice to competent in just 20 hours of focused effort. That's just **45 minutes a day for a month!** The common thread? Putting in the work.

Let's be honest—practice can be challenging. But understanding something and actually doing it are two entirely different things, and it's through action, not just knowledge, that you build real expertise.

Parallel parking is a great example of this. You could recite the textbook method flawlessly, yet still find yourself locked in a sweaty battle with a curb downtown. The gap between knowledge and action is vast. Just like parallel parking becomes second nature after countless attempts, any skill requires a journey of transforming theory into instinctive action.

Grasping new concepts might come quickly, tempting us to believe instant execution is possible. But the reality is that we need practice, feedback, refinement, and more practice. It's a roller coaster of embracing imperfections, making mistakes, adjusting, and trying again. While slow and sometimes uncomfortable, the end result is a powerful transformation.

How do we incorporate practicing new skills as a regular part of our LIVE BIG journey?

1. **Embrace Challenges.** Accept the initial wobbliness and expect stumbles. Celebrate the effort and risk-taking, not instant mastery. Reward yourself for venturing into new territory and sharpening your skills, even if your first steps are shaky.

2. **Prioritize Your Efforts.** Trying to master too many new skills at once is a recipe for burnout. Instead, zero in on one or two high-impact areas where you need the most improvement. Nail those, celebrate your wins, and then move on to the next. Progress happens faster when you focus your energy and let momentum build with each step forward.

3. **Dedicate Time.** Every day is an opportunity to level up—whether it's mastering new software, sharpening your interview skills, or developing your leadership abilities. But here's the thing: most people don't carve out time for real practice. Instead, they just "wing it," making slow, aimless progress. When you actually block time in your schedule to focus on skill-building, you start making real strides daily. And when you're consistently moving forward, you hit your goals faster than you ever thought possible.

I'm in the world of real estate—and if you are too, you know it can toss some real challenges your way. Maybe that last property you bought feels more like a money pit than a cash cow. But here's the thing: if you dedicate just a little time each day to analyzing deals, you'll quickly become a pro at spotting the next profitable gem.

Struggling to grab customers' attention with your business pitch? We've all been there! The great news is, with consistent practice on your presentation skills, you'll be locking in new customers like a magnet before you know it.

Feeling like your social media is a ghost town? The key is creating content that grabs attention. Set aside time each day to work on crafting irresistible hooks that pull your audience in. Before you know it, your Instagram will be buzzing with engagement.

We all start somewhere, and committing a little time each day can lead to big results. You've heard the saying, "Practice makes perfect," but let's forget about perfection—focus on progress instead. By intentionally carving out time in your schedule for growth, you're setting your future self up for success.

Be Loyal to Yourself

Ever feel like you're running on fumes some days? You're not alone. Let's face it, as female entrepreneurs, we're not only CEOs of our businesses, we're CEOs of our households, too.

We're the morning cheerleaders, making sure everyone gets out the door with homework, clean teeth, and hopefully, a touch of deodorant (yep, I raised two teenage boys). We're the lunch packers, the dinner preppers, the laundry-folding ninjas. We're the financial wizards, stretching every dollar and planning for tomorrow. We are, quite literally, the glue that holds our home lives together.

And then we walk into our businesses. Owner, manager, chief cook and bottle washer—it feels like it all falls on our shoulders. We're strategizing marketing campaigns, keeping the books in order, and making sure our clients are raving fans.

You and me? We're rock stars. We juggle commitments like a pro and always come through for the people we love and the businesses we've built. But here's the thing, friend: we cannot pour from an empty cup.

Have you noticed a pattern? We are constantly giving left and right to our families, our clients, our teams ... but what about ourselves? When was the last time you truly prioritized your own needs and well-being?

That's where I'm here to say: it's okay to put yourself first. It's not selfish, it's essential. Because a rested, recharged *you* is a better *you* for everyone in your life. So today, let's make a pact. Commit to showing up for yourself just as fiercely as you show up for everyone else.

Be loyal to yourself—you deserve it.

I first learned this lesson when I worked for Scripps Media. My role was to help small businesses leverage the power of digital marketing to grow their revenue. I came up with the vision behind the marketing campaigns, got my clients' buy-in, and my backend colleagues at Scripps took my ideas and brought them to life.

With an out-of-the box approach, I was creating real results for my clients. Top-producing strategist in the entire country? Check. Awards galore? Yep. Healthy commissions rolling in? Absolutely! I was a woman on fire, fueled by ambition and a deep love for helping clients thrive.

My boss, Stephanie Cooper, was a total gem—fun, supportive, and always in the trenches with the team. One Friday morning, I strolled into her office for our weekly one-on-one and settled into her cushy green chair, ready to soak up some high-fives for my latest client win.

But instead, she looked at me with concern and said, "Stacey, you're running on fumes. If you don't recharge, you'll burn out faster than a Black Friday sale."

Whoa. That was *not* the pep talk I was expecting. Sure, I was working seven days a week, but weekends? Who needs'em when there's a client to serve! I was laser-focused on being the go-to resource, snagging that #1 sales leader spot again, and building my financial fortress. It was thrilling!

But Stephanie saw something I didn't—I was overworking myself to the point of exhaustion. She saw the fire in my eyes dimming before I did, and she wasn't about to let that fire flicker out.

At the end of that Friday, I drove home with one mission: **recharge**. My body, mind, and yes, even my soul got a break that weekend—a break from the constant go-go-go. And recharging didn't require any day at the spa, fancy massages, or exotic body wraps. Instead, I reveled in the simple stuff. Lounging around in comfy clothes, taking my dogs for walks, and soaking up time with my family.

Now, it's not like these things were absent from my life before, but they were sandwiched between work tasks or squeezed into leftover pockets of time. This recharging weekend, though? My computer stayed shut, work emails politely ignored. Those two days were entirely mine, dedicated to the things that truly spark joy in me.

And to my surprise, the difference was night and day. Monday morning rolled around, and I practically skipped into work (okay, maybe a brisk walk). I plopped down in Stephanie's fluffy green chair (seriously, that thing was a cloud) and thanked her from the bottom of my heart.

Thanks to her, I finally understood the importance of recharging myself and prioritizing my own well-being, too. I had to realize that my loyalty couldn't just be for other people—I needed to start showing up for *myself* as well.

Create Self-Confidence by Being Loyal

There's more to loyalty than meets the eye. It's not just about doing what lights you up or spending time with your family (although those are pretty darned important, too). Being loyal to yourself means keeping your promises—big or small. It's about honoring your word. Even the words you say to yourself.

Self-confidence isn't some magic switch you flip on. It's a muscle you build, one rep at a time. And guess what? The strongest weights for that workout are the promises you make to yourself.

We all make little commitments to ourselves throughout the day, like "I'll tackle that project," or "I'll get to bed earlier tonight." But when you keep blowing off the things you say you're going to do, that inner voice starts to lose trust.

Here's the secret sauce: when you follow through on the words you say to yourself, even on the small stuff, you're building trust with the most important person in your life—*you.*

Remember, consistency is everything. When you follow through regularly, you're telling yourself, "I've got your back!" That's how you build a rock-solid foundation of self-trust. You stop being someone who just makes promises and become someone who delivers. Boom! Instant confidence boost.

Here are a few more things to keep in mind:

1. **Walk the Walk, Talk the Talk.** Remember that feeling of accomplishment when you finally do that thing you said was a priority and have been putting off ever since? Yeah, that's self-trust fuel right there. When your actions

are consistent with your words, you see yourself as someone with integrity, someone who lives by their values. Now **you** become a person that **you** can trust!

2. **Promises Made, Promises Kept.** This one seems obvious, but it's powerful. Every time you honor a commitment, you're proving to yourself that you're capable. When you're loyal to your word and keep the promises you make to *yourself*, the little voice inside you that used to doubt starts to get a lot quieter. And it's replaced by a strong "I've got this!" attitude.

3. **Building Your Trustworthy Resume.** The more times you keep your word, the more evidence you have of your own reliability. Imagine looking back at a long list of conquered goals and fulfilled promises. See? You're a total rock star! This track record strengthens your self-trust by showing yourself a clear pattern of your success.

4. **Decision-Making Confidence.** Being loyal to your word means taking ownership of your choices. You're consciously deciding what matters and following through. This builds confidence in your ability to make good decisions—and to have the guts to see them through. No more second-guessing, just steady progress toward your goals.

Being loyal to your word isn't just about keeping promises, it's about unlocking a vault of self-trust and confidence. It helps you believe in yourself, your choices, and your ability to conquer anything you set your mind to.

Measure Yourself by Your Own Ruler

Ugh, social media. We've all been there—scrolling through feeds, comparing ourselves to everyone else's picture-perfect lives. "Her post got way more likes," or "Her travel pics are amazing, and mine look like they were taken by a potato." It's a fast track to self-doubt. And the worst part? You're measuring your success with someone else's ruler.

Even the most confident people can get caught in that loop. It's so easy to question your own choices when you're focused on someone else's highlight reel.

But here's the truth: you don't need a million likes or a viral post to prove your worth. It all starts with the small promises you keep to yourself. Like finally starting that online course you signed up for months ago. Or committing to a daily meditation practice or even just taking yourself on a much-needed walk. Whatever it is, make a promise to yourself—and follow through.

Suddenly, you're not stuck comparing yourself to others. You're no longer relying on outside validation to feel good. Sure, other people's opinions can matter, but they don't define your confidence anymore.

The biggest confidence killers are breaking the promises you make to yourself and weighing your success against others' accomplishments. Guess what? You're unique, incredible, and on your own amazing journey.

Imagine looking in the mirror and seeing your biggest cheerleader staring back at you—the captain of your own personal hype squad! That's the magic of being loyal to your word. And the best part? That power is already within you, just waiting to be unleashed.

Use the Tools in Your Toolbox

Juggling a million things at once? Feeling like a plate spinner with way too many plates in the air? Here's some good news: there are some secret LIVE BIG tools you can use to conquer your commitments, master the art of getting things done, and stay loyal to your word—without losing your sanity!

Start by creating a schedule that actually works for you. Set realistic deadlines and prioritize your most important tasks. Time-blocking your calendar is like packing your backpack for an adventure. You know exactly what you need to bring and where you're headed, so you can avoid that overwhelmed feeling and have the energy to knock everything off your list.

Next, let's talk about teamwork. Yes, we're amazing women, but we're not superheroes—and we don't have to be. Delegating tasks to your team frees you up to focus on what you do best, lightening the load on your shoulders. Plus, who doesn't love a little support?

Speaking of support, building a strong network is key—it's like having your own personal cheerleading squad. Surround yourself with people who understand your goals and commitments. They'll encourage you, hold you accountable, and give you fresh perspectives when you're feeling stuck. Sometimes, all it takes is a pep talk from a friend to get you back on track.

And let's not forget, you can't pour from an empty cup. Taking care of yourself isn't selfish—it's essential! Get enough sleep, do things you love, and carve out some "me time." Think of it as giving yourself a superpower boost. When you're well-rested and energized, it's so much easier to stay focused and follow through on your promises.

When you LIVE BIG, it's about creating systems that work for *you*. These are just a few tools to help you manage the juggling act of life's commitments. Put them into action, and you'll feel less overwhelmed, more in control, and well on your way to becoming someone who's not just busy—but loyal to her word.

Prioritize Like a Boss

Alright, we've talked about the magic of keeping your word. It builds trust, makes you a rock star in everyone's eyes (including your own!), and proves you're someone who follows through. But, as we both know, life can be unpredictable. Even the most committed person can face unexpected challenges that make keeping their word tough.

Ever feel like your brain has ten tabs open, all screaming for your attention? Between running your business, handling client crises, juggling school drop-offs, planning meals, and somehow making sure the laundry gets done, it's no wonder you feel pulled in every direction.

When you're stretched too thin and your mind is scattered, keeping promises can feel impossible. You mean well, but when you're in full-on overload mode, nothing seems to stick.

The fix? Time to prioritize! Not everything gets a gold star, and that's okay. Start by making a list (because let's be real, lists are magic). Take a hard look at what's truly important. Be honest about what you can actually handle. You can't do it all. And guess what? You don't have to.

And here's the game-changer: it's okay to say no sometimes. Seriously, let me say that again. It's *okay* to say no. When you start prioritizing and focusing on the things that really matter, you'll not only keep your promises—you'll feel more in control, less stressed, and way more empowered to grow those beautiful Dream Seeds.

Give Yourself Grace

You set a goal, you're feeling amazing, totally crushing it ... and then BAM! Reality kicks in. Whether eating that irresistible slice of cake you swore you'd skip or choosing an extra episode of your favorite show over your workout. Suddenly, the guilt monster shows up, whispering all sorts of nasty things in your ear.

But here's the truth: we're not perfect. We're humans, not robots. In my business, we actually *celebrate* "relentless continuous improvement." It's all about learning, growing, and evolving—even from our missteps. So why are we so quick to tear ourselves down when we stumble on our own personal journeys?

Take me, for example. My New Year's resolution? "Lose those 20 pandemic pounds!" I was motivated, hitting the gym, eating clean ... and then, seemingly out of nowhere, I found myself face-to-face with a warm, gooey Crumbl Cookie. One minute I'm smashing a workout, and the next, I'm deep in a delicious sugary spiral.

Cue the instant guilt, right? But then I thought about it—would I berate a friend for having a treat? No way! So, why was I so hard on myself? That's when it hit me. The cookie wasn't a failure. It was just a small bump on the road to a healthier lifestyle.

Here's the real secret: grace is your ultimate self-care weapon. Let yourself off the hook! A slip-up is just that—a slip-up, not the end of the road. Dust yourself off, give yourself that pep talk in the mirror (because you're amazing!), and remember that progress isn't always a straight line. Celebrate every victory, big or small, and forgive yourself for those stumbles along the way.

The promises we make to ourselves are important, but so is self-compassion. Being loyal to yourself means stepping out of the "shame, blame, and judgment" zone and embracing something way better: grace, growth, and a little glitter (because who doesn't love a bit of sparkle on the journey to self-improvement?).

You're worth every promise you make to yourself—and when slip-ups happen, don't beat yourself up. Just pull out the grace card and keep moving forward!

Creating a Loyalty Loop

Loyalty isn't just a one-way street. It's a two-lane highway to success.

By now, you get the magic of loyalty—how keeping your word builds trust, boosts confidence, and helps you grow your Garden of Dreams. But here's the kicker: loyalty is a two-way street, and the best leaders know you've got to navigate both lanes to hit true success.

It's not only important to stay loyal to yourself, it's critical to show that same respect and commitment to the incredible people in your life—your family, friends, team, and even your vendors. These are the people who believe in you, have jumped on board your wild ride, and are helping you turn your big dreams into reality.

While it may feel natural to show love to our friends and family, how do we extend that same care to our team members and vendors?

- **Be a Shoulder to Lean On.** Life happens, and sometimes your team members (or vendors) might be going through challenges of their own. Being a supportive leader means showing up, listening without judgment, and offering a helping hand (or a listening ear and a vat of coffee, whatever the situation calls for).

- **Show Up, Always.** Be present and truly invested in the success of each of your team members. Offer support when they need guidance, and celebrate every win, big or small. A leader who shows up inspires loyalty. One who's checked out? Not so much. Your support matters, and it's the key to building a team that's just as committed as you are.

- **Create a Safe Space for Innovation.** Foster an environment where creativity is welcomed, and "what if" questions are met with curiosity, not skepticism. When people feel safe to experiment and share ideas, incredible things can happen. Encouraging that kind of openness is what fuels innovation and drives your team to new heights.

- **Be a Champion, Not a Critic.** Mistakes happen, even to the best of us. But remember, mistakes are stepping stones, not setbacks. When someone on your team slips up, be their champion, not their critic. Focus on finding solutions, not pointing fingers. Help them learn from the experience and come back stronger than ever. That's how you build a team that's resilient and ready for anything.

When people feel valued, supported, and empowered, they're more engaged, more productive, and willing to go that extra mile.

They become your problem-solvers, your partners, and your go-to crew on the path to success.

Loyalty is a two-way street, so show your team, your vendors, and your partners the same commitment you give yourself, your friends, and your family. Because let's be honest, building a dream team is pretty magical—and loyalty is the secret ingredient that makes it all work. It's time to lead with heart and create a loyalty loop that lifts everyone to new heights.

CHAPTER 8

STEPPING INTO YOUR BADASS SELF

A s a little girl, my skin was a stark white canvas, dotted with freckles. It wasn't the kind of complexion you'd see in those tanning lotion commercials, where girls showed off their sun-kissed, radiant skin. No, my skin was different—and as a young girl, I hated it.

When I hit my teenage years, I was determined to get that golden Coppertone tan I'd admired on TV. Every summer, my best friend Dawn and I followed the same ritual. By 10 a.m., I'd call to wake her up, and we'd grab our beach towels, slather on baby oil, and head out to the backyard. Armed with my boombox and a Steve Miller Band tape, we'd lay in the sun for hours.

Our mission was simple: 30 minutes on our backs, then flip and repeat. After each session, we'd rush inside to see if the sun had rewarded us with that coveted bronzed glow. Dawn would always be the winner, her skin effortlessly transforming into that perfect, sun-kissed tan we both dreamed of.

My results, however, were a whole different story. No matter how hard I tried, instead of that coveted golden glow, I'd end up as a flustered, bright shade of red, my freckles popping out like tiny islands in a sea of sunburn. While Dawn was effortlessly achieving her perfect tan, I was left with nothing but a painful reminder of how different my skin really was.

My mom, bless her heart, tried to get through to me early on. "There's something amazing about being unique," she'd say. "Your freckles and pale skin make you different, and that's beautiful." But let's be honest—I wasn't buying it.

I tried *everything* to achieve that bronzed goddess look. Baby oil? Total fail. Self-tanner? A streaky, orange mess. And in a moment of pure desperation (and perhaps a dash of teenage stupidity), I even convinced myself that spray butter—the kind you use on toast— would be my game-changing tool to sun-kissed skin. Spoiler alert: it wasn't. Sunburn city, here I come.

Of course, my mom was there every step of the way, offering her endless wisdom. "Stacey, those freckles are what make you special. Your fair skin is beautiful just the way it is." But did I listen at 16? Absolutely not. Because, well, teenager logic. She even warned me about sun damage, reminding me about Grandpa's skin cancer scare. Did I care? Nope. In my mind, sunbathing was life, conse- quences be damned.

Thankfully, wisdom does show up eventually. By the time I hit my late 20s, I had one of those lightbulb moments—Mom was right all along. My skin is exactly how it's meant to be, a masterpiece cre- ated by the good Lord above. So why fight it? Don't get me wrong, I still rely on full-coverage foundation to even out my complexion, and get a spray tan every once in a blue moon.

All in all, I've come to grips with my fair complexion. It's part of what makes me *me*, a constant reminder that I don't need to have a golden complexion to feel beautiful. Will I ever have that dreamy Coppertone tan? Nope. And honestly, I'd look downright weird with one.

The truth is, there's so much we *can* control—like nourishing our bodies with healthy food, taking those power walks that leave us energized, and maintaining a mindset that keeps us motivated. But our unique skin tones? That's a masterpiece already painted.

Learning to embrace my fair skin is a reminder that wasting energy trying to change things we can't control is not only exhausting, but risky too. Those frequent trips to the dermatologist to deal with basal cell carcinoma were the wake-up call I didn't know I needed.

No, I'm not a bronzed beach babe, and I never will be. But who needs that when you can glow as an ivory queen instead? Here's to SPF 50 and embracing what makes us unique—that's where true beauty lives!

Embracing Your Uniqueness in Business

As I ventured into business, I quickly realized that the same principle applies: just like every person's complexion, every business is unique. And that uniqueness? It's your superpower. Use it to your advantage and build your **Unique Selling Proposition (USP)**.

If you're running a business, ask yourself, "What truly sets me apart?" It can feel overwhelming, especially when competition is fierce. Forget worrying about your competitors, though—that's just wasted energy. Instead, focus on amplifying what makes your business unique. That's how you create real impact.

Whatever makes you different, own it, elevate it, and make sure the world knows about it.

Just like I eventually embraced my freckles and fair skin, you need to lean into and celebrate what makes your business one of a kind. In a sea of companies vying for the same customers, the real standouts are the ones that aren't afraid to show off their freckles.

Crafting Your Business's Unforgettable USP

Your Unique Selling Proposition (USP) is the clear, concise message that tells the world exactly why you're the perfect choice. It's the magic that turns you from "just another {insert your product/service here}" into *the* solution your customers have been searching for.

How do you craft this game-changing message? Grab a pen and paper because we're about to embark on a USP-creating adventure that will set your business apart from the rest!

Step 1: Know Your Tribe (Almost) Better Than You Know Yourself

Before you shout your message from the rooftops, you need to know who you're shouting to. That's where your ideal customer, your **target audience**, comes in. Here's the thing: they're not just faceless consumers. They're people with problems, dreams, and desires.

- **Discover Their Desires.** What are they hoping to achieve by using your product or service? Do they crave convenience, a touch of luxury, or a helping hand to solve a nagging pain point?

- **Unmask Their Fears.** What keeps them up at night (figuratively speaking)? Are they worried about quality, affordability, or simply making the wrong choice?

Step 2: Deep Dive into Your Competitive Landscape

Okay, you know your ideal customer, but what about the other folks selling similar things? Time to delve into the world of your competitors.

- **Scout the Territory.** What are they doing well? What are their weaknesses? Are there any gaps in the market they're not addressing? This intel will help you position your USP strategically.

Step 3: Unleash Your Inner Badass

Now for the fun part: identifying what makes your business special! Here's where you brainstorm all the things that set you apart.

- **What Are the Things That Make You a Badass Business Owner?** Maybe it's the knowledge you've gained through years of experience in the field, or maybe it's the incredible journey that led you to this point. It could even be your unique educational background that sets you apart. Whatever it is, write it down! These are the special ingredients that make your business stand out, and sharing your story can be a powerful asset.

- **What Makes Your Badass Business Shine?** Is it the amazing way you streamline the process for your customers, making everything super smooth and easy? Maybe you source your products with a focus on sustainability or fair trade practices, because you care about the impact you make. Or perhaps your secret weapon is your team—a bunch of passionate experts who light up every day, ready to tackle any challenge!

Whatever sets you apart, write it down! These are the super-powers that make your business unique and special, and they're definitely worth shouting about. So go on, brag a little—you deserve it!

Putting It All Together

Now that you've gathered all your intel, it's time to write your USP! Here's a handy formula to get you started:

> We help [ideal customer] by [solving their problem] so they can [achieve desired outcome] without [pain your ideal customer wants to avoid].

Here are some examples to spark your creativity:

- **For a Local Bakery:** "We help busy families enjoy delicious, homemade treats without the baking hassle, so they can create lasting memories around the dinner table without the mess, the time crunch, or the stress of fixing complicated recipes."

- **For a Dog Walking Service:** "We give busy pet parents peace of mind with reliable and loving dog walks, so their furry friends get the exercise and attention they deserve without the guilt of leaving them cooped up, the stress of rushing home, or the worry that they aren't getting the care they need."

- **For a Freelance Graphic Designer:** "We empower small businesses with eye-catching and affordable designs, so they can stand out in a crowded marketplace without breaking the bank, sacrificing quality, or getting lost in a sea of competitors."

Your USP shouldn't gather dust on some forgotten document. Test it out! Share it with your target audience, see how they respond, and refine it based on their feedback.

Remember, your USP is a living, breathing thing. As your business grows and evolves, your USP should, too. Keep it fresh, keep it relevant, and most importantly—keep it aligned with what makes your business stand out.

Handy Tips for Crafting Your USP

In addition to crafting a USP for your company, take it a step further—develop specific USPs for each of your products or services. Picture your business as a brilliant star in the night sky, distinct and glowing with its USP shining bright. Now, imagine each of your products or services as smaller stars orbiting around it, each with its own USP, creating a constellation of irresistible offerings.

This stellar lineup of USPs not only makes your business stand out, but it also sparks upsells and keeps your customers coming back for more. Don't stop at just one USP for your brand—give each of your products a shining USP of their own, and watch your business soar!

Let's say you're an artist looking to promote both your custom artwork and your mural painting services. Here's how you can stand out with clear, compelling USPs for each offering.

- **Custom Art:** "We help homeowners and interior designers bring their unique vision to life with personalized, one-of-a-kind artwork, so they can transform their space into a true reflection of their style without settling for generic, mass-produced pieces or struggling to find the perfect fit."

- **Mural Painting:** "We help businesses and homeowners elevate their spaces with custom mural paintings, so they can create a bold, unforgettable atmosphere that reflects their personality and brand without the hassle of generic designs or the limitations of off-the-shelf artwork."

Ready to Take Your USPs to the Next Level?

Head over to **LiveBigWithStacey.com/resources** and download the **USP Glow-Up Guide** to start crafting messaging that not only cuts through the noise but also draws in your dream customers like a magnet. With just a little effort and these handy tips, you'll have your products and services flying off the shelves in no time!

Making Decisions Like a Boss (Because You Are One!)

You've nailed down your uniqueness and crafted stellar USPs for your business and each of your products or services. But there's one more critical power move to master: **strategic decision-making.** Think of yourself as an architect designing a skyscraper. Every blueprint, every decision—from the foundation to the finishing touches—determines the strength and success of your structure.

Running a business is the same! Strategic decisions are your blueprint, guiding your company toward its ultimate vision. These choices shape everything from the products you create to the team you build, and even how you engage with your customers. Nail these decisions, and you'll set the foundation for long-term success.

But making strategic decisions can be tricky. They involve weighing risks and rewards, analyzing data, and sometimes taking a leap of faith. Even the most seasoned entrepreneurs can get tripped up. Any of these sound familiar?

- **The Analysis Paralysis Trap.** You get bogged down in research, overthinking every option and ending up paralyzed by indecision. While action without a plan is reckless, planning without ever taking action keeps you motionless!

- **The Fear of Failure Monster.** Every decision carries some risk. But letting this fear hold you back keeps your business stagnant. Even the most successful entrepreneurs make mistakes. The key is to learn from them and keep moving forward.

- **The Shiny Object Syndrome.** A new marketing trend emerges, or a competitor makes a bold move, and suddenly, you're tempted to abandon your carefully crafted strategy for the "next big thing." Stay focused on your long-term vision, or you'll find yourself constantly shifting without making real progress.

The LIVE BIG Strategic Decision-Making Framework: Your Path to Greatness

Alright, enough about obstacles! Let's shift gears and get you equipped with some tools to make *boss-level* decisions. Whether you're deciding on that next investment property or thinking about launching a new service line for your business, this framework will help you generate ideas and make the right call.

Step 1—Set the Stage for Success

Before diving in, define what decision needs to be made.

- **Identify the Problem or Opportunity.** What challenge are you facing, or what exciting new possibility is on the table? Define it clearly so you know exactly what you're dealing with.

- **Set S.M.A.R.T. Objectives and Outcomes.** What are you aiming to achieve with this decision? Make sure your goals are Specific, Measurable, Achievable, Relevant, and Time-bound. And here's a power move—give yourself a deadline. Whether it's in an hour, by the end of a meeting, or weeks down the road, setting a clear timeframe to make your decision will help you avoid getting stuck in analysis paralysis.

Step 2—Gather Intel

Knowledge is power!

- **Research and Collect Data.** Dive in and gather everything you can—market insights, customer feedback, financial reports—anything that brings clarity to your decision. The more informed you are, the better.

- **Consult Your A-Team.** Don't hesitate to tap into your trusted circle—your team, mentors, mastermind group, or industry experts. Getting multiple perspectives can open up new ideas and lead to brilliant solutions you might not see on your own.

Step 3—Brainstorm Like a Boss

Now comes the fun part—generating creative solutions.

- **Think Outside the Box.** Push yourself to explore a range of options, even the unconventional ones. Try setting a timer and see how many ideas you can come up with in a set amount of time—it adds a fun challenge to the process. And don't forget to invite your A-Team to join the brainstorming session! More minds, more ideas, more possibilities.

- **Evaluate Your Options.** Take a close look at each option. Break down the pros and cons, and think through both the short-term and long-term impacts. If you're feeling stuck or need another perspective, don't hesitate to bring in a trusted team member, mentor, or coach to help you weigh your options. Two heads (or more) are always better than one.

Step 4—Make the Best Choice Possible

For recovering perfectionists like me, this step can be the hardest.

- **Think Like a Futurist.** Check in with your GodRod and imagine how your decision could unfold in different scenarios, considering the best- and worst-case outcomes. Trust your intuition and, with the information you have, choose the path with the most favorable potential. This forward-thinking approach will help guide you to the best option.

- **Make the Decision.** It sounds simple, but delaying the decision is where many get stuck. Perfectionism sneaks in, or you convince yourself you need more info. Remember,

"Done is better than perfect," and "Everything is figure out-able." Make the decision and move forward—progress is the goal!

Step 5—Take Action

You've wrestled with the options, weighed the risks, and made the tough call. Now, it's time to transform that decision into action. Here's how:

- **Develop an Action Plan.** Think of this as your roadmap to success. Map out the specific steps needed to implement your decision, breaking it down into smaller, more manageable tasks. Who needs to do what, and when? Assigning clear ownership and deadlines keeps everyone accountable and ensures your plan stays on track.

- **Communicate Clearly.** Don't let your decision get lost in translation. Clearly communicate your decision and the rationale behind it to everyone involved. This is a critical step that often gets overlooked. If your decision requires changes from your team, explain the "why" as well as the "what." Understanding the reasoning behind the decision helps your team feel aligned and invested in its success.

Step 6—Grow From Every Decision: Lessons Learned Lead to Future Wins

Your decision-making journey doesn't end here. This is an ongoing process where you learn and grow with each experience.

- **Monitor and Evaluate.** Keep a watchful eye on the progress of your decision. Is it achieving the desired results you set in Step 1? If not, be ready to adapt and adjust your approach. Remember, strategic decisions are like steering a car—sometimes you need to adjust the route based on unexpected detours. Stay flexible, and be ready to shift gears if new information or circumstances arise. It's all about staying focused on your destination while adapting along the way!

- **Learn from Every Step.** Take time to reflect on the entire decision-making process. What went well? Pinpointing these areas will sharpen your approach and set you up for even better outcomes in the future. Think of each choice as a learning opportunity that strengthens your strategic decision-making muscle.

Strategic decision-making is a skill that gets stronger with practice. The more you use this framework, the more confident and clear you'll be in navigating whatever comes your way. And here's the best part—this isn't just for business! You can use it in every area of your life to open new doors, solve problems, and most importantly, LIVE BIG!

CHAPTER 9

YOUR HIDDEN UNIVERSE
OF POWER

Imagine a control center more powerful than any computer you've ever seen. That's your brain—a three-pound universe of complexity packed neatly inside your skull. Here's a glimpse into the incredible things your brain does, all while you're busy conquering your day:

- **The Maestro of Your Body.** Your brain conducts a full orchestra of organs. It tells your heart to beat, your lungs to breathe, and your digestive system to keep things moving smoothly. It even regulates your temperature, ensuring you stay cool on a hot day and warm on a chilly one.

- **The Mighty Defender.** Your brain is your personal bodyguard. It runs your immune system, constantly on the lookout for invaders like viruses and bacteria. When a threat is detected, it deploys a powerful army of white blood cells to fight them off.

- **The Master Repair Crew.** Accidents happen, even on a microscopic level. But your brain has a built-in repair crew, constantly fixing tiny tears in your muscles and tissues.

It's like having a team of the world's tiniest construction workers toiling away 24/7 to keep you in tip-top shape.

- **The Symphony Conductor of Movement.** Every move you make, from picking up a pen to dancing the night away, is powered by your brain. It sends complex signals to your muscles, telling them exactly how to contract and relax to create smooth, coordinated movements.

- **The Gatekeeper of Your Senses.** The sights, sounds, smells, tastes, and textures you experience all travel through your brain. It interprets the raw data from your senses and creates the rich tapestry of your world.

- **The Engine of Your Emotions.** From the soaring joy of a win to the crushing weight of grief, your brain is the master behind every emotion you feel. It processes everything you experience and generates the feelings that color your life.

- **The Spark of Genius.** Every brilliant thought, creative breakthrough, and problem-solving moment originates in your brain. It allows you to learn, adapt, and invent, constantly pushing the boundaries of human potential.

And that's just the beginning! Your brain is also involved in things like faith, consciousness, and instinct. It's a complex and mysterious marvel, even to the most dedicated scientists.

Here's the truly empowering part: the potential within your brain is limitless. Whether you're leading a Fortune 500 company, losing weight, launching your dream business, or working toward any other goal, your brain has the power to make it happen.

But tapping into that potential is sometimes way easier said than done.

Say Hello to Your "State of Mind"

Pick any state in the USA, and let's pretend for a few minutes that the state you selected is actually your brain. Close your eyes and picture your "state"—it's chock full of more than 86 billion citizens. That's a huge population, right?! And just like us, every single one of those citizens has a job to do, working hard day in and day out to keep everything running smoothly.

Now, here's something unique about this state—its citizens live and work *really* close to one another. It's almost like they're constantly huddled together, whether they're in a bustling metropolis, a mid-size city, or even a tiny rural town where the only thing downtown is a single stoplight. No matter where they are, they're all tightly connected!

The last characteristic of these 86 billion citizens? They're talkers—some are loud and outspoken, while others have a softer voice. But no matter the volume, they're constantly communicating with one another. And here's the kicker—they're not just chatting with their next-door neighbors; they're connecting with people all across the state, constantly sharing information.

How do they communicate? Through information highways that connect all the population centers and people. There are roads of every size—massive highways, narrow one-lane roads, and everything in between. Cars travel along these imaginary roads, transporting information from one place to another, keeping everything connected and running smoothly.

Those 86 billion residents? They represent the neurons in your brain. Yep, there are nearly 90 billion of these nerve cells constantly talking to each other, making everything happen in your body—from breathing to walking, laughing, and talking.

And those information highways? They're called **synapses**. Some are like six-lane freeways, carrying a *ton* of traffic. These are the connections you use all the time—the well-worn paths in your brain's landscape.

Then, there are the smaller, one-lane roads. These are the synapses carrying information you don't use as often. And when you're learning something new? That's like a dirt road waiting for concrete to be poured, ready to become a well-traveled route.

The more you travel a certain brain-road (by learning a new skill or practicing a habit), the wider and stronger that road becomes (the synapse strengthens). Conversely, if you stop driving down a particular road (an old habit you're trying to break), it might eventually become overgrown (the synapse weakens).

Your brain keeps the well-traveled paths (strong synapses) and deactivates the unused ones (weak synapses) to stay efficient. But the exciting part is that you can always build new roads and strengthen existing ones!

This gives a whole new outlook on the phrase "State of Mind," don't ya think?!

Next up, we're diving into powerful strategies to unlock the full potential of your brain. Get ready to turn it into a goal-crushing machine! You've got this, and your brain is about to work *for* you in ways you never thought possible. Let's go!

Rewiring Your Brain for Change

Every single day, your mind is firing off a ton of thoughts—some researchers say between 12,000 and 60,000! But here's the surprising part: most of those thoughts (around 85%) are actually negative. And to top it off, 95% are just reruns of yesterday's mental movies. Not exactly the recipe for an awesome life, right?

But remember all that cool stuff we just covered about synapses—those information highways in your brain? Well, here's the good news: you have the power to change them. Ready to hear how?

Think of your negative thoughts—the ones that whisper doubts and fears, telling you you're not good enough or that success is just a dream. These negativity champions are probably cruising around your brain in a flashy red Corvette, zooming down a six-lane highway at breakneck speed. They're loud, they're obnoxious, and they're hogging all the space.

Now imagine your positive thoughts—the ones that make you feel unstoppable and light a fire under your dreams. These empowering superstars are probably stuck sputtering along a dusty, single-lane dirt road in a 1920s Model T. They barely have a voice, and they're getting nowhere fast.

But here's the secret weapon: **you** are the driver of these cars! Through this incredible ability called neuroplasticity, you can take control of the traffic flow in your brain. Imagine ditching the old red Corvette that's been hauling your negative thoughts around and trading in that outdated Model-T carrying your positive thoughts for a sleek, shiny green Ferrari!

Sounds like something straight out of a *Fast and Furious* movie, doesn't it? Well, buckle up, buttercup, because neuroplasticity is real, and it's about to transform your life!

Neuroplasticity in a Nutshell

Next, I want you to think of your brain as the most amazing lump of clay ever. Just like Play-Doh®, it's constantly molding and changing based on what you do and experience.

Neuroplasticity is the scientific term for this mind-blowing ability. It means your brain can form new connections and pathways throughout your entire life, not just when you're a kid.

How Does This Brain Magic Work?

We've already established that your brain is a bustling hub of billions of neurons, and these little guys and gals talk to each other constantly, sharing information through electrical signals. The more they chat, the stronger their connection becomes. Neuroplasticity allows these neural highways to constantly reroute and rebuild themselves, depending on what you're learning or experiencing.

Let's say you decide to learn a new language, like Spanish (¡Hola!). As you practice those tricky conjugations and master those new vocabulary words, your brain is busy forming brand new connections between neurons. Pretty cool, right?

Neuroplasticity in Action: Real-Life Examples

Here are some everyday situations where you can see neuroplasticity working its wonders:

- **Learning a New Skill.** Remember the first time you tried to ride a bike? Wobbly wheels, scraped knees, and all? But with practice, those neural connections strengthened, and now you can probably hop on and ride without a second thought. That's neuroplasticity in action!

- **Bouncing Back from Injury.** Sometimes, life hits us with unexpected challenges, like an injury or illness. But here's the incredible part—your brain has the power to heal and adapt. Through rehabilitation and therapy, other areas of the brain can step in and take over for the injured parts, helping you regain lost abilities and come back stronger than before.

- **Breaking Free from Bad Habits.** We all have them—those pesky vices that hold us back. But guess what? Neuroplasticity can be your secret weapon! By consistently replacing those bad habits with positive ones, you can literally rewire your brain's pathways. The more you practice the good stuff, the easier it becomes.

For me, discovering neuroplasticity was a game-changer. By learning how to build new connections in my brain, I could focus on inner growth, which led to incredible outer changes. My thoughts shifted, my confidence soared, and my life transformed in ways I never imagined.

The best part? You can do this, too! It's never too late to start harnessing the power of neuroplasticity, and this amazing ability is with you for life. By adopting simple habits—like learning new things, getting active, and staying positive—you can literally rewire your brain for a future that's brighter and more fulfilling than ever before.

What are you waiting for, superstar? It's time to unleash the incredible potential that's already within you! Let's get this brain magic party started!

CHAPTER 10

LIFE-CHANGING BRAIN EXERCISES

Before we dive into these awesome brain exercises, I have to give a huge shout-out to the incredible John Assaraf, the Brain Whisperer himself. His teachings completely reshaped my thinking (and my life), and I'm forever grateful!

Now, I want you to brace yourself because these exercises might sound a little ... well, wacky. You might even think they're straight out of a woo-woo convention. But trust me on this—do them anyway.

These are some of my personal favorites, and I still use them all the time. They've become my secret weapons for unlocking my mind and achieving the kind of success that once felt impossible.

My biggest tip? Practice these brain exercises every day. Memorize the steps so they become second nature. Then, when a challenge pops up, you can whip these powerful tools right out of your back pocket and conquer anything. Let's get your brain fired up and ready to create your best life ever!

Power Breaths

Take six deep breaths. With each deep breath, say to yourself, "I breathe in [insert noun]; I breathe out [insert noun]."

What's awesome about this exercise is that you can insert any nouns you want and tailor it to any situation:

- Screaming kiddos have you ready to lose your cool?
  - "I breathe in calmness; I breathe out anger."

- Feeling foggy about a big decision and not sure what your next move should be?
  - "I breathe in clarity; I breathe out confusion."

- Prepping for a big presentation and feeling nervous?
  - "I breathe in confidence; I breathe out overwhelm."

- Your crazy calendar has got you feeling anxious?
  - "I breathe in tranquility; I breathe out anxiety."

As you breathe in, hold it for a second, savoring that feeling of peace washing over you. Then, slowly exhale through pursed lips, like you're blowing out a birthday candle. Imagine all the stress and tension leaving your body with that exhale.

Not only does this exercise allow you to reshape the way you're feeling but also tells your brain what you're taking in and what you're letting go of. This helps you counter the natural reaction your brain has to situations triggered by stress.

It's like hitting the pause button on your stress reaction and giving your body a chance to unwind. Pretty freakin' cool, right?!

Triple D (Discover, Decide, Do)

Close your eyes and picture yourself in your ultimate chill zone. Maybe it's a sandy beach with crystal-clear turquoise water lapping at your toes, perhaps you're swaying gently in a hammock nestled in the peaceful woods. Whatever your happy place looks like, imagine yourself there.

Take six Power Breaths, picturing the changes in your body with each inhale and exhale.

1. Inhale—*I breathe in calmness.* Feel your body start to relax. Exhale—*I breathe out stress.* Imagine stress literally leaving your body.

2. Inhale—*I breathe in focus.* Feel your mind starting to clear. Exhale—*I breathe out overwhelm.* Picture the feeling of overload melting away.

3. Inhale—*I breathe in peace.* Feel a sense of serenity wash over you. Exhale—*I breathe out anxiety.* Imagine those worries dissolving into thin air.

4. Inhale—*I breathe in calmness.* Feel your body continuing to relax. Exhale—*I breathe out stress.* Picture the stress drifting away.

5. Inhale—*I breathe in focus.* Feel your mind completely clear. Exhale—*I breathe out overwhelm.* Feel your overload melting away.

6. Inhale—*I breathe in peace.* Feel a sense of complete calmness. Exhale—*I breathe out anxiety.* Picture your worries floating away like a puff of smoke.

Now, take a moment to check in with yourself. How does your body feel? Are your shoulders still tense, or are they starting to loosen up? Is your mind calmer, or are there still some nagging worries buzzing around? Don't judge yourself. Just be aware.

Discover. Ask yourself: What is my intention for today—or in this moment? Do I want to stay stuck in this stress spiral? Or do I want to feel calm, focused, and empowered?

Decide. You have the power to choose. Choose peace, choose clarity, choose calmness. Choose to be in control. Pick something powerful and positive.

Do. Once you have your intention set, take one action step toward achieving it. Right now, don't wait. Immediate action is key. It moves you out of the reactive zone and into a proactive state where you're the boss of your emotions.

Practice this exercise and watch your ability to stay calm and focused skyrocket. Stress doesn't have to dictate your day. Breathe, discover your desired intention, make a choice, and then take action—it's that simple!

Switch Gears

You have emotions, but you are not your emotions. They're triggered by your subconscious and create the feelings you experience.

Think of it like this: imagine you're a Hollywood A-list actress. You've just landed a HUGE role, the kind that pays $10 million and comes with Oscar buzz. The catch? You have to flawlessly switch between emotions, voices, and behaviors on a dime.

Ready to practice? Let's do this!

Stand tall, chin up, and give me your biggest, brightest smile. Hold it for 60 seconds and *feel* the positive energy run through you.

Now, let's switch gears. Recall a time when you experienced a significant loss. Allow yourself to fully feel that memory and embrace the sadness it brings. Be sad. Feel the weight of that sadness, how it affects your body. What does your chest feel like? What about your arms and legs? Be aware of how sadness *feels*.

Okay, time to switch gears. It's time to get angry. Think of something that really makes you mad. Bring up that feeling and notice how it affects your body. Be aware of what your body *feels* like with anger running through it.

Switch gears. Picture yourself achieving a major goal, absolute elation washing over you. *Feel* that surge of happiness, the excitement bubbling up. Notice how your body responds—chances are, your breath deepens, muscles relax, and a smile naturally appears.

This exercise shows you have the power to flip from negative thoughts to positive ones, quite literally in two seconds. You just did it right here in this exercise! Who knew, right?! The key is staying aware of your emotions and how you feel; then, *actively* and intentionally choosing the emotion that feels best.

The power is within you. You're not stuck on this emotional rollercoaster. Take breaks throughout your day, check in with yourself, and consciously choose how you want to feel. You're in the driver's seat.

Now, for some real-life practice. Take 90 seconds to reflect on this newfound power. Picture yourself achieving a goal that sets your heart on fire. Let that feeling of success wash over you.

This is the LIVE BIG energy, my friend! Let it fuel your every move. Remember, you're not your emotions. You're the master of your own destiny, and you get to choose how you experience life.

Gratitude Dial

Alright, let's center ourselves and unlock some serious gratitude power! Take six Power Breaths. Inhale slowly through your nose, feeling your belly expand. "I breathe in clarity; I breathe out confusion," (or whatever nouns you want to insert). Hold for a beat, savoring that sense of calm. Exhale slowly through pursed lips, letting go of any tension with each breath.

Feeling relaxed and present? Perfect! Now, picture a dial right in the center of your chest, like the dial on a stove burner. This is your personal **Gratitude Dial,** and it controls the intensity of an imaginary **Gratitude Flame** burning inside you.

Now, think of something you're incredibly grateful for. It could be anything—a supportive spouse, a business opportunity, even your amazing ability to breathe deeply.

As you focus on this feeling of gratitude, imagine turning the dial on your chest clockwise. Feel the Gratitude Flame inside you get bigger and brighter with each tick of the dial.

Take the next few minutes to fully immerse yourself in gratitude. Feel the love and appreciation rise up within you. As you continue to breathe calmly, notice how the warmth of the Gratitude Flame fills your entire being.

When you focus on gratitude, you're activating powerful chemicals in your brain. The more you train your brain to find things to be grateful for, the easier it becomes. Just like turning your Gratitude Dial, it's a superpower you can develop!

No matter what challenges life throws your way, cultivating gratitude is a game-changer. It helps you refocus, reframe your thinking, and find strength in the simple things.

Now, for the next two to three minutes, let your Gratitude Dial go wild! Turn it all the way up. Think about everything you're grateful for, big or small. Let those feelings turn that Gratitude Flame inside you into a blazing inferno of positivity. The more you turn that dial, the brighter your flame will burn, illuminating your life with joy and abundance.

Cultivating gratitude is a daily practice. Keep coming back to this exercise and watch your inner flame shine brighter and brighter each day!

The Experience Coin

Ever feel like life throws you a curveball, and it knocks you off your feet? Here's the truth: every situation has two sides, a good and a bad. And the key is **YOU** get to choose how you see it! This exercise will help you train your brain to see the empowering side, the one that fuels your success.

Everything in the universe has an opposite, an up for every down, an inside for every outside. Even emotions and experiences.

Every experience has a positive and a negative, and you get to choose how you perceive these opposites.

Take six Power Breaths, inhale slowly through your nose, filling your belly with air. Feel the coolness travel down your throat and into your lungs. Hold that air in for a second, savoring that feeling of peace.

Then, exhale slowly through pursed lips, like you're blowing through a straw. Imagine all the stress and tension leaving your body with each breath. Remember to repeat your Power Breath nouns, "I breathe in [insert noun]; I breathe out [insert noun]," with each inhale and exhale.

Now, picture yourself holding a coin in the palm of your hand—this is your **Experience Coin.** One side is shiny gold, engraved with "Positive + Empowering." The other side is dull and gray, marked "Negative + Disempowering." Here's the best part: YOU decide which side lands face up!

Here's how it works: throughout the day, catch yourself when you judge a situation. Is a conversation leaving you feeling drained? Maybe an email drips with negativity. That's your cue to flip the coin!

As you envision the coin spinning, ask yourself empowering questions: "What's the hidden gem in this challenge? How can I use this to become even stronger?"

With each empowering question, the coin lands on the shiny, positive side. Just like that, you've intentionally shaped your perspective—and with it, reclaimed your power!

Ready to practice? Close your eyes and picture that Experience Coin in your hand. Feel the cool metal and the weight of your power. This coin, this amazing perspective, is yours. Tuck it into an imaginary pocket that's always with you, ready to pull out whenever you need it.

In any challenging situation, take out the coin, give it a flip, ask yourself the questions above, and choose the empowering side. Your brain is a feeling machine. The perspective you assign to an experience determines how you feel about it, which then affects your actions. Choose empowering perspectives, and watch your life transform.

Let's feel this shift in your brain. Close your eyes and repeat this declaration with me:

> From this moment forward, I empower myself through heightened awareness. I intentionally select thoughts, emotions, behaviors, and meanings that energize me and empower me.

Repeat it twice more, feeling the positive energy building with each declaration.

Repeat this affirmation two more times, letting the power of your words sink in.

Finally, for the next minute, just be present. Focus on your breath, feel your body, and let your mind wander toward positive thoughts and achieving your goals.

Cloud 9

Set a timer for nine minutes, find a cozy spot, and close your eyes. Start with six Power Breaths and say, "I breathe in calmness; I breathe out stress." Let any tension melt away from your body with each exhale.

Now, imagine yourself gently sinking into a big, fluffy white cloud—softer than the plushest marshmallow you can dream of. Take flight in the sky and feel the weightlessness as you drift along, and picture the smile on your face. Isn't that amazing? Take a moment to really soak in the feeling of pure freedom.

Let the gentle breeze tickle your hair as you float higher and higher. There are no rules here—you can drift over sparkling oceans, soar above majestic mountains, or even visit that dream vacation spot you've always wanted to see. Just let your imagination (and your cloud) take flight!

The whole time, keep focusing on that feeling of weightlessness, of letting go of everything that might be weighing you down. Let your worries drift away like wispy clouds on a windy day.

Daydream, explore, and let your mind wander wherever it wants to go. Maybe you'll see a friendly dolphin in the ocean, or maybe you'll build a sandcastle on a beach made of stardust. Whatever it is, embrace the joy and wonder.

When your nine-minute mini-vacation is over, gently let your cloud drift back down to earth. Take a few moments to wiggle your toes and come back to the present. Then, grab your journal and jot down anything interesting you saw or experienced on your cloud adventure. You might be surprised by the insights you discover!

When you let your brain run wild with creativity and wonder, something truly magical happens. It's like giving your mind a workout at the coolest gym ever, and guess what it's doing? Building brand new pathways!

These new neural highways allow you to develop fresh behaviors, like a ninja mastering a new fighting style. The more you do these nine-minute brain workouts, the more your brain adapts and grows, making it easier than ever to achieve those awesome goals you've been dreaming of! Pretty cool, right?

CHAPTER 11

WHY YOUR BRAIN LOVES COMFORT ZONES (BUT HATES ACHIEVEMENT)

E ver set a New Year's Resolution with fierce determination, only to find yourself back at square one a few weeks later? You're not alone. Our brain is our body's most amazing organ, but it can also be our own worst enemy when it comes to achieving the outcomes we're seeking. Why? Because your brain is a survival machine at its core. It prioritizes two things above all else:

1. **Safety.** Your brain's number one job is to keep you safe—physically, emotionally, and mentally. It's wired to remember every close call (think "lions, tigers, and bears—oh my!") and avoid anything that feels risky. (Even if that risk isn't real … more on that later.)

2. **Efficiency.** Your brain juggles a million tasks every second, from blinking to complex problem-solving. To save energy, it loves familiar routines and ingrained habits. It's like having an "autopilot" mode for daily life to conserve energy.

The way your brain prioritizes safety and efficiency is great for survival, but not always for achievement. Here's why:

- **The Comfort Zone Trap.** Your brain's focus on safety and efficiency can make change feel threatening. Anything new or different gets flagged as a potential risk. This is why starting a business can trigger fear, or why a delicious dessert might win out over a healthy salad—your brain craves the familiar "safe" option.

- **The Habit Monster.** Your brain loves efficiency, so it relies heavily on autopilot mode. This is useful for things like brushing your teeth, but not so helpful when you're trying to break a bad habit or build a new one. The familiar autopilot keeps kicking in, pulling you back to your old ways.

So what does this mean for you? It means that unlocking your best potential might require you to do a little reprogramming! The key to success lies in understanding your brain and using its power to your advantage.

Meet the Tiger and the Elephant

Picture yourself standing at the edge of a lush, untamed jungle. Sunlight filters through the dense canopy, casting dappled shadows on the vibrant green foliage. Exotic birds call out from hidden branches, while the air is thick with the sweet scent of blooming flowers and the rich, earthy aroma of damp soil. But this isn't just any jungle—this thriving wilderness is a reflection of the intricate landscape of your mind.

Here, in this vibrant chaos, roams a magnificent tiger. Its stripes, sharp and focused, represent your logical, analytical side. This is the voice of ambition, the part of you that sets bold goals, crunches numbers with precision, and charts the most strategic path forward in your business. It roars with the power of "I will LIVE BIG! I'm ready to create the business I want and the life I deserve!" This, my friend, is your **conscious mind**, the fierce, powerful tiger at the heart of your inner jungle.

But lurking in the distance is another animal—a giant. One that's incredibly strong, a powerhouse of intuition and habit, capable of incredible feats. It's your **subconscious mind**, the strongest creature in the land—the African elephant. While it seems harmless, this elephant can be unpredictable and sometimes even destructive.

The elephant runs on emotions, habits, and deeply ingrained beliefs. And despite its massive size, it's incredibly fast and sneaky. It's the strongest force in the land, capable of shaping your actions and decisions without you even realizing it.

Your tiger might be consciously planning a calculated product expansion in your business, looking to develop a new exercise ritual, or visualizing your next investment, but the elephant (your subconscious mind) is already making decisions based on past experiences and emotional triggers. It acts like a filter on your reality, influencing how you see the world and respond to situations. Your elephant quietly guides your decisions without you even noticing.

This elephant is also a creature of habit. It loves routine and efficiency and especially loves running on autopilot. Think about putting on lipstick or tying your shoes—do you really need to use any brain energy for tasks like that? But this preference for routine and efficiency can be a double-edged sword.

While these automatic routines are great for everyday tasks, they can also make it tough to break bad habits or build new ones. The elephant loves the familiar and resists change, even if that change is what you truly need.

And because your elephant is so strong, it can easily trample your tiger's ambition.

But here's the best part. Your inner elephant doesn't have to be the enemy. In fact, once you understand its power, you can transform it into your greatest ally. This wise giant can be a source of incredible creativity, intuition, and problem-solving skills.

Imagine your conscious mind (tiger) as the driver, setting the direction with ambition and focus, and picture your subconscious mind (elephant) as the powerful engine, using its strength and wisdom to propel you forward. Together, they can be an unstoppable force, helping you conquer the jungle and achieve anything you set your mind to.

Neural Coherence and Cognitive Dissonance

When I was a kid and the summer Olympics came on, my mom would be glued to the TV—her favorite sport to watch? Synchronized swimming. I remember sitting in front of the "boob tube" as she used to call it, watching all those women in matching caps and bathing suits performing in perfect unison, their arms and legs splashing and creating a beautiful ballet choreographed just for the water.

Now, imagine what would happen if the neurons firing away inside your head could work together in perfect harmony? Like synchronized swimmers, each neuron would be doing its own individual job, but all contributing to a stunning outcome.

That's the magic of **neural coherence**. It's when your brain waves synchronize, creating a unified rhythm—almost like a water ballet conducted by your brain. This beautiful collaboration allows your conscious mind (the tiger) to work seamlessly with your subconscious mind (the elephant).

Imagine your curious tiger is in the dark of night, holding a spotlight that illuminates a small area in front of you. This is what you're consciously aware of at any given moment. But your elephant? It's carrying a massive, detailed map of the entire jungle, even though you can't see it. It holds everything you've ever experienced, learned, and felt.

In neural coherence, the tiger and the elephant team up. The spotlight illuminates the details right in front of you, but with the added benefit of the elephant's map. You see the big picture, how everything connects, and gain a deeper understanding of the world around you. It's like having a built-in GPS for life.

What Are the Superpowers of Neural Coherence?

Laser Focus. When your brain waves are in sync, you can filter out distractions like a boss. Imagine being able to concentrate on that important project without the constant ping of social media notifications or the neighbor's lawn mower interrupting your flow. Neural coherence allows you to tune out the noise and lock in on what matters, giving you laser-like focus to stay on task and get things done.

Creativity Explosion. Ever feel stuck in a rut, creatively speaking? When your conscious and subconscious minds are in perfect harmony, information flows freely. Suddenly, you're brimming with fresh ideas and innovative solutions to problems that once seemed impossible to solve.

Emotional Master. Feeling overwhelmed or stressed? Neural coherence can be your emotional lifeguard! When your brain waves are synchronized, you can manage your emotions more effectively. Think of it as learning to surf your emotions—riding the waves with control instead of being thrown around by them. Neural coherence promotes feelings of calm, well-being, and inner peace.

Intuition Amplifier. Ever have a gut feeling that turned out to be right? That's your intuition (a.k.a. your GodRod) whispering wisdom from your subconscious. Neural coherence strengthens the connection between your conscious and subconscious minds. You tap into a deeper knowing, making better decisions and feeling more in tune with yourself.

When you're in neural coherence, just like in synchronized swimming, where every movement is coordinated, your brain naturally ensures that every thought is aligned with every action. This harmony allows you to navigate challenges, focus intensely, and take strategic actions without second-guessing yourself. With neural coherence, you're not fighting the current—you're flowing with it, making progress feel effortless and easy.

The Elephant in the Room: Your Tiger Isn't in Control

Now, here's the kicker: the tiger and the elephant don't always see eye-to-eye. The tiger craves change, thrives on adventure, and is always ready to take on the next big challenge. Picture it wanting to hike up a mountain, eager for the thrill. Meanwhile, your wise elephant—holding the map, seeing the steep climb and potential risks—is saying, "No way!"

This inner clash is what we call **cognitive dissonance.** It's when your conscious mind (the tiger) is all about progress, while your subconscious mind (the elephant) clings to the comfort of routine. It's that push-and-pull between wanting more and staying safe in what's familiar.

And guess who usually wins that battle? Yup, the elephant! Remember, it's the strongest animal in the land.

When you try something new, it can feel unfamiliar and uncomfortable for your subconscious, which just wants to conserve energy and stick to what's safe. So, what does it do? It throws doubts, fears, and roadblocks into your path.

This dissonance can be draining. You get frustrated, and achieving your new vision seems insurmountable. You retreat back to your Comfort Zone, letting the elephant win, and forgetting about the change you were once so excited about.

But why is our elephant (subconscious mind) pressing those "brakes" in the first place? More often than not, it's because of **limiting beliefs.**

Understanding Limiting Beliefs

Limiting beliefs are the stories we tell ourselves that hold us back—like invisible barriers standing between us and what we're truly capable of achieving. They're often rooted in doubt or fear, but once we recognize them, we can break free and move forward with confidence.

These constraining thoughts emerge from your subconscious mind, which controls about 95% of your behaviors and decisions.

It stores memories, experiences, and learned behaviors, creating a huge reservoir of information that influences your daily life. Unlike the conscious mind, which processes information logically and analytically, the subconscious mind is more associative and emotional, linking feelings and experiences to create patterns that guide your actions.

Where do limiting beliefs come from? They're often formed during early childhood, a time when the subconscious mind is highly receptive and impressionable. These beliefs can stem from various sources, including:

- **Family and Upbringing.** The attitudes and beliefs of your parents or caregivers play a huge role in shaping how you see yourself and the world around you.

- **Societal and Cultural Influences.** Cultural norms and societal expectations can plant seeds about what's "possible" or "acceptable," limiting your vision of what you can achieve.

- **Personal Experiences.** Traumatic events or even repeated failures can leave you believing you're not capable or worthy of achievement or prosperity.

- **Education and Media.** Messages from the education system or media can reinforce limiting beliefs about intelligence, beauty, and what defines success.

The Paradox of Sudden Wealth: A Case Study in Limiting Beliefs

Imagine a pair of sunglasses permanently fused to your face. They tint your vision, filtering the world through a specific color scheme.

This is what our beliefs do. They are the distorted lenses through which we interpret life, influencing everything we think, say, and do. These beliefs, often formed in childhood or through past experiences, become ingrained patterns in our minds, shaping our reality.

When we think of lottery winners, we often picture them living out their wildest dreams without ever having to worry about money again. Yet, research reveals a startling truth: **most lottery winners end up bankrupt within a few years.** Why? The answer lies in a disconnect between their **external environment** (sudden wealth) and their **internal beliefs about themselves** (self-worth).

Take Jack Whittaker as an example; he won a staggering $300 million lottery jackpot. Instead of a happy ending, his story is one of tragedy. Whittaker's pre-existing limiting beliefs—perhaps about his own financial responsibility—couldn't reconcile with the vast influx of wealth. His subconscious mind, in a twisted attempt to restore balance, self-sabotaged him through reckless spending and bad decisions. Remember **cognitive dissonance?**

This example illustrates the power of limiting beliefs to keep us trapped in familiar patterns, even when our reality drastically changes.

Limiting Beliefs: The Silent Saboteur

Here's the insidious nature of limiting beliefs: they operate in the shadows, shaping our choices without our conscious awareness. They can manifest as:

- **"I'm Not Good Enough."** This belief can cripple your confidence and hold you back from pursuing your dreams.

- **"Failure Is a Sign of Weakness."** This discourages taking calculated risks, hindering personal growth.

- **"Money Is the Root of All Evil."** This creates a negative association with wealth, sabotaging your ability to achieve financial abundance.

These are just a few examples, and the list goes on. Until you identify and dismantle these limiting beliefs, you'll continue repeating the same patterns, unknowingly holding yourself back from the success you deserve.

The Path to Freedom: Rewriting Your Story

The good news is, limiting beliefs are not set in stone. You have the power to rewrite your internal narrative. Here's how:

1. **Shine a Light on Your Beliefs.** The first step is awareness. Pay close attention to your self-talk and the stories you tell yourself about what you're capable of.

2. **Challenge the Narrative.** Once you've spotted a limiting belief, question it. Ask yourself, "Is this really true? Is there any real evidence to support it?"

3. **Replace and Reinforce.** Swap out that critical inner dialogue for empowering self-talk. Create affirmations that align with your new beliefs—write them down, say them out loud daily. Over time, these affirmations become your new internal script, replacing the negative narratives that once held you back.

Building a New Reality

This isn't a one-time fix. It's a continuous process of self-discovery and rewiring your neural pathways. Say your new beliefs out loud right after you write them down every day, visualize yourself achieving your goals, and surround yourself with supportive people who believe in you.

The world is a reflection of your beliefs. By shattering the glass ceiling of limitation, you open yourself to a world of possibilities, a life brimming with the vibrant colors of your true potential. Now, take a deep breath, ditch the dusty glasses, and step into the grand adventure that awaits!

Taming Your Limiting Beliefs

Now that you've met your tiger and your elephant, it's time to introduce another character in this incredible brain jungle—the inner critic, a gorilla named "Grumpy Greg."

Greg specializes in limiting beliefs, and he loves to stir up negativity, doubts, and anxieties. Picture him sitting in a cage on top of your right shoulder, and when he's locked up, Grumpy Greg is harmless.

Here's the thing, though: when your elephant, the master of routine, is running the show, it tends to leave the cage door wide open for Grumpy Greg. Suddenly, you're hit with waves of negativity, and achieving your goal or what you "want" feels impossible.

But remember, *you* have the power to keep Grumpy Greg locked away. How do you do it? Use my top five tips for taking charge and becoming a master at taming those limiting beliefs.

1. **Catch Grumpy Greg in the Act.** The first step is awareness. Notice when those negative thoughts creep in. Visualize Grumpy Greg getting back in his cage. Then lock the door.
2. **Challenge the Narrative.** Don't accept limiting beliefs or disempowering thoughts as truth! Question them. Is there

evidence to support it? Probably not. Often, it's simply fear masquerading as a fact.

3. **"I Am Done With That."** This is another powerful strategy I learned from John Assaraf. Once you've identified a limiting belief or a negative thought, declare, "I am done with that!" Say it with conviction, stuffing Grumpy Greg in his cage and slamming the door.

4. **Affirm Your Power.** Replace the limiting belief with an empowering one. Instead of "I can't," say "I'm learning." Shift "I don't deserve it" to "I am worthy of ...." Repeat these affirmations like mantras, reprogramming your subconscious mind for success.

5. **Progress, Not Perfection.** There will be slip-ups, times when Grumpy Greg gets loose. That's okay. Don't beat yourself up. Acknowledge he's out of the cage, grab him, stuff him back in, then lock the door with your "I am done with that" statement. This way, you stay in control and keep moving forward. And always remember to give yourself grace; there's no shame or blame if Grumpy Greg escapes.

You are the zookeeper of your incredible brain. Now that you're aware of your tiger (your conscious mind), your elephant (your subconscious), and even Grumpy Greg (that inner critic), you hold the key to creating the life you've always dreamed of.

By understanding these fascinating creatures in the jungle of your mind, you can learn to harness their strengths and keep negativity in check. It's time to unlock your brain's full potential and step into a world of *limitless* possibilities. You've got everything you need to LIVE BIG!

CHAPTER 12

THE SECRET TO BUSTING FEAR AND STRESS

Picture yourself standing at a crossroads. One path is familiar, comfortable—it's the route you've traveled many times. The other is shrouded in mist, full of unknowns, but brimming with adventure and possibility. *This* is the power of choice. It's the magic ingredient that empowers you to design the life you truly want.

But here's the scoop: choice isn't like a genie in a bottle granting effortless wishes. It's a muscle—one that gets stronger the more you use it. The more aware you become of your thoughts, feelings, and desires, the easier it becomes to recognize opportunities to choose.

Think of awareness as the first spark. It lights up the landscape of your life, revealing countless paths in front of you. With this new awareness, you get to *build* your choices. You can stick to the safe, familiar route, or you can summon the courage to step into the unknown. Every choice, whether big or small, shapes your journey.

And here's where things really get exciting: as you build choices, you create intention. Intention means consciously deciding how you want to think, feel, and act. It's about setting your life's compass and aligning your choices with your deepest desires. This is where your power to LIVE BIG truly takes root!

For example, let's say you're aware that you often feel anxious and overwhelmed. Now, you have a choice. You can continue down the path of worry, or you can choose to build an intention of calmness and focus. This intention then inspires further choices: practicing meditation, setting boundaries, or delegating tasks. Each choice, informed by your intention, empowers you to create a more peaceful and productive life.

> NOTE: Anxiety can also be caused by a chemical imbalance in the brain. I want to be clear—I'm not discounting this at all. If you're dealing with overwhelming anxiety, it's important to seek help from a medical professional. Your health always comes first!

Intention is the bridge between awareness and action. It transforms your choices from random occurrences into deliberate steps toward your outcomes. It's the difference between drifting through life and actively navigating toward your dreams.

Here are some ways to cultivate awareness, build choices, and solidify your intentions:

- **Practice Mindfulness.** Pay attention to your thoughts, feelings, and bodily sensations without judgment. This heightened awareness empowers you to make conscious choices.

- **Identify Your Values.** What matters most to you? Aligning your choices with your core values gives your intentions a strong foundation.

- **Visualize Your Desired Outcomes.** Picture the life you want to create—your Garden of Dreams in full bloom. This powerful visualization helps guide your decisions, making it easier to choose the actions that bring you closer to that vision.

- **Embrace Self-Compassion.** We all make mistakes. Forgive yourself and learn from them. This allows you to refine your intentions and make better choices moving forward.

The power of choice is already within you. By cultivating awareness, creating options, and setting your intentions, you become the architect of your own life. You're no longer standing passively at the crossroads—you're actively choosing the path that leads you to your most fulfilling, purpose-driven life. Take a deep breath, embrace the possibilities ahead, and start crafting your extraordinary adventure. The journey is yours to create!

Eliminating Fear and Stress

Fear—the most destructive four-letter "F-word." We've all felt it. It's the stomach knot before a big presentation, the clammy hands on a first date, or the panicked gasp when a (gulp) spider darts across the bathroom floor. Fear, my friend, is a powerful and complex emotion. But before we dive into how to tame it, let's first understand its origin story.

Inside your brain is a central control room called the *amygdala*, and inside it is your elephant dressed up as a security guard who's on constant high alert. Its sole mission? To keep you safe. It scans your environment, both physical and mental, looking for potential threats. A suspicious shadow on the street? "Danger!" A looming deadline?"Danger!"A creepy, 8-legged hairy insect?"RED ALERT!"

Remember, though, your elephant doesn't have logic, and it can't tell the difference between a bear in the woods and your imaginary fear of public speaking. It simply throws up the metaphorical stop sign, triggering the release of stress hormones like adrenaline and cortisol. These hormones are like emergency responders, surging through your body to prepare you for fight or flight.

This fear mechanism served us well back in the caveman days, but in our modern world, where the biggest threat during your day might be forgetting a meeting, this constant state of high alert can be exhausting. It can also hold us back from living our best lives, from the **ability** to LIVE BIG.

Imagine that dream business you've always wanted to launch, but the fear of failure keeps you stuck in your current, comfortable (but unfulfilling) job. Or maybe you dream of writing a book, but the fear that no one will read it holds you back, so you stick to journaling for yourself. These are just a few ways our imaginary fears can become roadblocks, keeping us from living a truly BIG life.

Here's the good news: while our elephant in a security guard uniform can be a little *too* protective, we can learn to manage its overreaction. The more we understand how our fear response works, the more we can take charge of it—instead of letting it control us.

Now that we've discussed fear, let's dive into another sneaky saboteur: **stress.**

How Stress Halts Our Success

We've all been there—drowning in deadlines, swamped with responsibilities, that knot of tension in your stomach growing tighter with every passing minute. Stress, my friend, is a part of life. But when it becomes a chronic companion, it can steal the joy from your journey and leave you feeling like you're trudging through mud instead of scaling the mountains of your dreams.

How does stress hold us back from Living BIG? Let's take a closer look at 10 of its sneaky tactics:

- **Brain Drain.** Ever feel like your brain has gone on vacation under pressure? Stress can cloud your thinking, making it hard to focus, remember things, and make sound decisions. It's like trying to solve a puzzle with blurry vision—not exactly a recipe for success.

- **Productivity Plummet.** When you're stressed, productivity takes a nosedive. Simple tasks feel monumental, and mistakes become more frequent. It's like wading through quicksand—every step feels like a struggle.

- **Motivation Meltdown.** Chronic stress can lead to burnout, that feeling of utter exhaustion where even the most exciting goals lose their luster. Suddenly, that dream project feels like a chore, and the fire in your belly dwindles to a faint ember.

- **Body Blues.** Stress doesn't just mess with your mind, it wreaks havoc on your body, too. Headaches, stomachaches, trouble sleeping—these all become unwelcome visitors, draining your energy and forcing you to slow down when you just want to push forward.

- **Mental Health Matters.** Stress can be a major trigger for anxiety and depression. These conditions can make it even harder to focus, manage your time, and chase your dreams with the necessary gusto.

- **Impulse Overload.** When stress hits, healthy coping mechanisms can fly out the window. You might find yourself reaching for that extra slice of cake or hitting snooze a few too many times. These behaviors might offer temporary relief, but they ultimately hinder your progress.

- **Social Siberia.** Feeling stressed? You might find yourself withdrawing from friends and family, the very people who can offer support and encouragement. This isolation can make it even harder to bounce back from setbacks and keep moving forward.

- **Communication Catastrophe.** Stress can turn even the most articulate communicator into a fumbling mess. Misunderstandings and conflicts can arise, creating tension in your personal and professional life.

- **Creativity Block.** Say goodbye to your inner artist. Stress narrows your focus, leaving little room for the expansive, creative thinking that fuels innovation and problem-solving. It's like trying to paint a masterpiece with a paintbrush dipped in mud.

- **Sleepless Struggles.** Stress can make catching those precious Zzz's a distant dream. And let's face it, without proper sleep, your brain and body can't function optimally. It's a vicious cycle—stress keeps you awake, and lack of sleep makes you more stressed.

Now here's the good news: you're not powerless, and you can loosen the grip that fear and stress have on your life. Imagine waking up feeling energized, your mind clear and focused, ready to tackle your goals with a renewed sense of purpose. That's the power of living free from the clutches of fear and stress.

And remember, self-care isn't selfish; it's necessary. By taking care of yourself, you're better equipped to handle life's challenges and pursue your dreams with passion and resilience.

Fear- and Stress-Busting Activities

We've explored some of the ways that fear and stress can hold you hostage; now, it's time to discover the arsenal of fear and stress busters waiting to be your allies on your journey.

A powerful toolkit for cultivating inner peace and boosting your resilience starts with meditation and journaling. Here's a mindfulness meditation to get you through each day:

A Guided Mindfulness Meditation for Your Inner Sanctuary

Find a Comfortable Position. Sit or lie down in a quiet space where you won't be interrupted. Close your eyes gently, or soften your gaze if that feels more comfortable. Take a few deep breaths, inhaling slowly through your nose and exhaling completely through your mouth. Feel the rise and fall of your chest with each breath.

Notice Your Body. Gently scan your body from head to toe, starting with the top of your head. Are there any areas of tension or discomfort? Acknowledge them without judgment, and simply allow them to be there. Move your awareness down your neck and shoulders, your arms and hands. Notice any sensations in your back, your stomach, your legs, and your feet. Take a moment to appreciate your body, this amazing vessel that carries you through life.

Focus On Your Breath. Let your breath be your anchor. Notice the cool air entering your nostrils with each inhale, and the warm air leaving your mouth with each exhale. Count your breaths silently if that helps you stay focused. If your mind wanders, gently bring your attention back to your breath, without judgment.

Observe Your Thoughts. As thoughts arise in your mind, simply observe them like clouds drifting across the sky. Don't get caught up in their content. Label them as "thinking" and let them pass without judgment.

Embrace the Present Moment. Let go of any worries about the future or regrets about the past. Bring your awareness to the present moment. Notice the sounds around you, the feeling of your breath, the sensations in your body. Be fully present in this moment, right here, right now.

Find Your Sanctuary. Picture yourself in a peaceful place where you feel safe and relaxed. This could be a real place you've been to, or a place you create in your mind. Notice the details of your inner sanctuary—the sights, sounds, smells, and sensations. Feel the peace and tranquility of this place wash over you.

Spend Some Time in Your Sanctuary. Allow yourself to be fully immersed in the tranquility of this peaceful place. Breathe deeply and let go of any lingering tension or stress. This is a time for you to simply *be*, to reconnect with yourself on a deeper level.

Gently Return. When you feel ready, slowly bring your awareness back to your body. Wiggle your fingers and toes, and take a few deep breaths. Open your eyes gently. Carry the feeling of peace and tranquility from your sanctuary with you throughout your day.

Mindfulness meditation is a skill that takes time and effort to develop. Don't get discouraged if your mind wanders—simply bring your attention back to your breath and start again. Be kind to yourself and enjoy the journey.

Journaling

Think of your journal as a trusted friend—a place where you can unload all your worries, fears, and frustrations without judgment. Scribbling them down can help you see them for what they are— just thoughts on a page, not monsters under your bed.

But journaling isn't just about venting. It's also a powerful tool for positive self-reflection. As you write, you might discover hidden strengths and creative solutions to future stress monsters. It's like having a pep talk with your most awesome self, and who wouldn't want that?

The Fear & Stress Buster Journal Template coming up next is your tool for tackling fear head-on and turning stress into a stepping stone for growth. Use it to check in with yourself, reframe your mindset, and regain control. Pair it with the visualization practice, and you'll start noticing real changes in how you face life's challenges.

Want this template at your fingertips? Download it at:

LiveBigWithStacey.com/resources

Or scan the QR code:

Fear & Stress Buster Journal Template

Date: _____

1. Fear Check-In

- What am I feeling afraid of today? (Be specific.)
- How does this fear manifest in my body (racing heart, tight muscles)?
- What is the worst-case scenario I'm imagining?

2. Reality Check

- How likely is it that this worst-case scenario will actually happen? (Be honest!)
- Are there any steps I can take to prepare for or prevent this scenario from happening?
- What evidence do I have to suggest things might not be as bad as I fear?

3. Reframing the Fear

- What is another way to look at this situation?
- Could this fear be a sign of a hidden opportunity?
- What positive outcome could arise from facing this fear?

4. Action Plan

- What small, manageable step can I take today to address this fear?
- Who can I reach out to for support?
- What positive affirmations can I use to combat this?

5. Stress Relief Techniques

- What relaxation techniques can I practice today to de-stress (meditation, deep breathing, yoga)?
- What healthy activities can I engage in to manage my stress (exercise, spending time in nature)?
- What activities bring me joy and relaxation?

Bonus

- **Gratitude Boost.** Reflect on three things you're grateful for today.
- **Visualization.** Spend a few minutes visualizing yourself successfully overcoming your fear.

Be kind to yourself as you work through these exercises. Journaling is a personal journey, so feel free to adapt this template to fit your needs.

Get Your LIVE BIG 90-Day Momentum Maker

Don't forget that the LIVE BIG 90-Day Momentum Maker is here to help you push past your barriers and take control of your life. This isn't just an ordinary planner. It's your go-to tool for turning fear into fuel and stress into strategic action.

Each day, you'll map out clear, actionable steps to move forward. The journaling activities will help keep you grounded, empowered, and focused on what really matters. It's time to stop letting fear hold you back—and start building the life you deserve.

**Grab your copy now by scanning the QR code
or visiting the link below.**

LiveBigWithStacey.com/momentum

Time Management: Master Your Days and Conquer Your Goals!

Feeling overwhelmed by your to-do list? Effective time management is key to reducing stress. Techniques like creating daily schedules, prioritizing tasks, and setting realistic goals can help you feel more in control and prevent you from feeling swamped.

Remember, *you* are the master of your mind *and* your schedule!

Set a timer for five minutes and do a brain dump of all the things you need to accomplish today. Next, prioritize them using the Eisenhower Matrix. This handy tool, created by the incredible Stephen Covey (author of *The 7 Habits of Highly Effective People*), helps you categorize your tasks based on urgency and importance. Think of it as a roadmap to a less stressed, more productive you!

Write the Matrix as a big box, divided into four squares. On the X-axis is importance (the tasks that align with your long-term goals and dreams), and on the Y-axis, we have urgency (those tasks screaming for immediate attention). Let's dive into each square and see where your tasks belong:

	IMPORTANCE	
U **R** **G** **E** **N** **C** **Y**	**Do First! Important & Urgent** This is where true emergencies live—critical deadlines, pressing issues that can't wait. Imagine you're in IT and suddenly face a tech failure, or picture yourself driving down the highway when you hit a pothole and get a flat tire. These fiery tasks deserve your immediate attention, so tackle them first!	**Schedule It! Important & Not Urgent** Ah, this is where your long-term dreams reside! These tasks contribute to your Dream Seeds, but they don't have a screaming deadline attached. This is where you might find things like writing that book you've always dreamed of, or practicing that new skill. These tasks are the ones that truly propel you forward, so schedule dedicated time for them in your calendar—treat them like precious appointments with your future self!
	Delegate It! Urgent & Not Important This is the land of interruptions—emails that ping at the worst moment, or favors for others that sidetrack you from your own goals. While these tasks feel urgent, they often don't contribute to your Dream Seeds. The key here is to delegate whenever possible and become a master of saying "no" politely but firmly. Your time is valuable, so spend it wisely!	**Delete It! Not Important & Not Urgent** These tasks are basically clutter for your mind. Got unproductive meetings cluttering up your calendar? Cut them out. While it might seem harmless (or even a good idea), these tasks can steal precious time from what truly matters. Identify these time-drainers and eliminate them from your list—your future self will thank you!

Now that we've nailed down your most critical tasks, it's time to approach your day with strategy and intention. It's time to plan it!

Daily Planning

1. Top Three Priorities

- What are the three most important things you MUST accomplish today? (Focus on the top row of the Eisenhower Matrix.)

2. Schedule Breakdown

- Block out dedicated time slots for each of your top three priorities.
- Allocate time for other important tasks, meetings, appointments, etc.
- Include buffer time for unexpected interruptions or tasks.
- What are other blocks of time that are important to you? Be sure to put them on your calendar (exercise, family time, self-care).

3. The LIVE BIG Power Hour

- Schedule one hour each day dedicated to your most important Dream Seeds. Spend just 60 minutes a day tending to your Garden of Dreams, and watch your progress unfold in ways that will amaze you.

4. Energy Levels

- Pay attention to your natural energy levels throughout the day. Schedule your most demanding tasks during the times when your focus is at its peak and save the lighter tasks for those moments when you're feeling a bit tired or "less sharp." This simple shift can maximize your productivity and help you stay in your flow!

Bonus Tips for LIVE BIG Time Management

- **Minimize Distractions.** Turn off notifications, silence your phone, and find a quiet space to focus on your work.

- **Embrace "Batching."** Group similar tasks together to streamline your workflow and stay in the zone. Or, try batching all your meetings on specific days to free up other days for problem-solving or creative thinking. This approach keeps you focused and gives you the mental space you need to tackle your biggest challenges.

- **Take Breaks.** Schedule short breaks throughout the day to avoid burnout and maintain focus.

- **Celebrate Your Wins.** Acknowledge your accomplishments, big or small!

- **Be Flexible.** Unexpected events happen. Review and adjust your plans as needed.

- **Prioritize Self-Care.** Schedule time for activities that nourish your mind, body, and spirit.

Building a Support System

Humans are wired for connection. We thrive on the warmth of a loved one's embrace, the laughter shared with friends, and the feeling of being truly heard and understood. And here's the best part—this deep need for connection isn't just a need to feel good in the moment; it's a powerful tool for busting through fear and stress!

Think of it like this: when fear or stress takes over, it's easy to get stuck in your own head, with worries swirling around like a never-ending storm (yep, that's Grumpy Greg running wild!). But when you talk to a trusted friend, family member, coach, or therapist, it's like opening a window and letting in a fresh breeze of perspective and support. That outside help can be just what you need to get Grumpy Greg back in his cage where he belongs!

Sharing your burdens doesn't magically make them disappear, but it can lighten the load significantly. Just the act of talking things out can help you process your emotions and gain a clearer understanding of what's causing your stress. And let's face it, sometimes the best stress relief is a good laugh with a friend who "gets" you.

Here's the magic of human connection: when you share your fears and anxieties with someone you trust, they can offer validation. They can remind you that you're not alone in this, that these feelings are normal, and that you have the strength to overcome them. Plus, they might offer a different perspective on an issue or a new way to approach a situation that you might not have considered on your own.

Don't underestimate the power of simply feeling heard. Sometimes, just having someone listen without judgment or advice can be incredibly therapeutic. It allows you to release some of that emotional pressure and feel lighter.

The next time you're feeling stressed or overwhelmed, reach out! Talk to a friend, call a family member, or schedule a session with a coach or therapist. Connection is a superpower—use it to chase away fear and stress, and step into a calmer, more supported version of yourself. You deserve it!

Sleep Hygiene

A good night's sleep is like a magic potion for both your mind and body! When you prioritize sleep, you're actually giving yourself a powerful stress-fighting tool.

Imagine trying to fight an ugly stress monster on zero sleep. You're sluggish, your reflexes are slow, and your brain is fried. But when you get that restful night's sleep, you wake up feeling like a superhero. Your mind is sharp, your body is energized, and you're ready to tackle anything that comes your way, stress monster included.

And you don't need a magic spell to unlock the power of sleep for stress relief. By creating a regular sleep schedule (going to bed and waking up around the same time each day, even on weekends!), you train your body to know when it's time to wind down. Plus, a relaxing bedtime routine can be like a warm blanket, lulling you into a peaceful slumber. And ditching the screens before bed? That's like giving your brain a mini-vacation from the constant stimulation of the digital world.

I absolutely prioritize sleep. In fact, for a normal day at home, I typically go to bed around 7 p.m. Yes, most people think I'm crazy, but for me, it's perfect. I'm not saying you need to go to bed that early, but experts say the average person should get between 7 and 9 hours of sleep each night. Me? I roll out of bed at 4 a.m. Why? Because that's when my mind is sharpest, and I love to wake up when it's quiet in my house, enjoy my coffee, learn something new, and turn on my creativity.

Healthy Diet

Nourishing your body with the right kinds of fuel is an important tool in your stress-busting arsenal.

Your body is an amazingly sophisticated machine, and just like any machine, it needs the right fuel to run smoothly. When you fill it up with sugary snacks and processed foods, it's like running your car on dirty gas—it sputters, stalls, and definitely isn't ready for a high-speed chase (against fear and stress!). But when you feed your body with a balanced diet full of fruits, veggies, and healthy fats, it's like giving it premium fuel. Your mood gets a boost, your energy levels soar, and you feel more resilient and capable of handling whatever comes your way.

Now, here's the scoop—I love a good chocolate chip cookie or bag of potato chips, and I'm certainly no expert nutritionist. But eating healthy doesn't have to be complicated or bland! There's a whole world of delicious, nutrient-packed foods out there that can fuel your body and help you feel your best. It's about discovering what makes you feel energized and ready to take on the day.

Each day, verbalize your commitment to ditch the sugary snacks and processed junk, and fuel your body with the good stuff. Record what you eat each day and journal how you feel. A healthy, happy body results in a healthy, happy mind!

Living BIG with Less Stress

Fear and stress management is a skill that needs practice. Be patient with yourself, celebrate your victories, and don't be afraid to seek professional help if needed. With a commitment to self-care and stress management, you can cultivate inner peace, unleash your potential, and LIVE BIG with a heart full of joy and a mind free from worry.

Transforming Your Habits

When we LIVE BIG, we are *actively* working on ourselves, driving continuous improvement in our businesses and in our lives. In order to do this, we need to understand the incredible power of habits! These are the tiny routines, both good and bad, that weave themselves into the fabric of our days. They shape who we are, but guess what? They don't have to hold us hostage.

Over the next few pages, we'll dive into the world of habits and walk through practical strategies to break free from those negative routines that keep us stuck. And even better, you'll learn how to build powerful new habits that fuel your journey to help you step into your best life.

Habits: The Blueprint of Our Lives

Have you ever noticed how you can drive to work or brush your teeth without really thinking about it? That's the power of habits. They make life easier, helping our elephant (subconscious mind) conserve energy by automating routine tasks. While this can be incredibly useful, it also means that both disempowering and negative habits can become deeply ingrained in our lives.

Habits are behaviors we repeat so often they become automatic. Our elephant creates these patterns to help us navigate daily life more efficiently. This process is governed by a loop consisting of three parts: the cue (or trigger), the routine (the behavior itself), and the reward (the benefit we gain from the behavior). Understanding this loop is key to changing our habits.

The Habit Loop: A Cup of Java and the Science of Rewiring

Ever find yourself mindlessly brewing that cup of coffee each morning, counting down the seconds to that first jolt of caffeine? That's *dopamine* at work—the sneaky brain chemical that gives you that feel-good hit and keeps you coming back for more.

Here's what happens: your brain sets up a habit loop with a trigger, routine, and reward.

- **Trigger**: You wake up in the morning.
- **Routine**: You head downstairs, see the coffee pot, and brew a cup.
- **Reward**: That first *delicious* sip!

When that coffee hits your lips, dopamine floods your brain, making you feel satisfied. The more you repeat this loop, the stronger it gets, and before you know it, you're running on autopilot.

How do you break free from the habit loop? Forget relying on willpower—it's no match for your elephant, where your habits live. The secret is to disrupt the habit loop before it even starts!

- **Recognize the Trigger.** While you can't avoid waking up in the morning, you *can* spot the trigger in your routine— like seeing the coffee pot. If you're the only one who drinks coffee, tuck the coffeemaker away in a closet. If others in the house drink it too, try moving the coffee pot to a new spot that's out of sight when you wake up.

- **Insert a New Response.** Instead of pouring, get moving! Take a walk, hit the gym, or turn on your favorite music and have a mini dance party (air guitar totally encouraged!).

These new actions break the old loop and create a fresh association. Now, waking up leads to movement and fun—a much healthier and energizing reward for your awesome brain.

Here's another example of a habit loop: checking social media.

1. **Trigger:** The feeling of tiredness or boredom in the afternoon.

2. **Routine:** You reach for your phone and unlock it, the familiar gesture a signal to your brain that stimulation awaits.

3. **Reward:** The barrage of notifications, likes, and updates triggers a surge of dopamine, making you feel momentarily engaged and entertained.

Again, the reward cycle reinforces the connection between the trigger (tiredness/boredom) and the routine (checking social media). The more you repeat this loop, the stronger the connection becomes, making it automatic. That's why you might find yourself reaching for your phone on autopilot; your brain is craving that dopamine hit.

Next time that afternoon slump hits, try this:

1. **Recognize the Trigger.** Notice the feeling of tiredness and identify it as the trigger for your social media browsing.

2. **Insert a New Response.** Get up and grab a healthy snack or a refreshing glass of water. Take a few deep breaths or do some stretches at your desk. You can even step outside for some fresh air.

These new responses interrupt the established loop and create a new association between the trigger (tiredness) and a healthier response (nourishment, relaxation, or even a mini-break).

It's all about baby steps. Start by introducing small disruptions to your routine, and celebrate your victories, no matter how tiny. Every time you interrupt the loop and choose a new response, you're rewiring your brain for positive change.

The next time you feel an ingrained habit creeping in, remind yourself—you have the power to break free.

Empowering Habits vs. Negative Habits

Empowering habits are positive behaviors that enhance our lives and help us grow. These habits contribute to our well-being, productivity, and overall happiness. Here are some examples:

- **Exercise.** Regular physical activity boosts our mood, energy levels, and overall health.

- **Healthy Eating.** Consuming nutritious foods fuels our bodies and minds, leading to better performance and longevity.

- **Reading.** Engaging with books expands our knowledge, enhances creativity, and improves cognitive function.

- **Mindfulness Practices.** Activities like meditation and journaling help us stay present, reduce stress, and cultivate self-awareness.

- **Outcome Setting.** Setting specific outcomes and continuously cultivating our Garden of Dreams keeps us motivated and focused on our goals and aspirations.

Negative Habits

Negative habits, on the other hand, are behaviors that detract from our well-being and hinder our growth. These habits can drain our energy, lower our self-esteem, and keep us stuck in unproductive cycles. Some common negative habits include:

- **Procrastination.** Delaying important tasks can lead to stress, missed opportunities, and feelings of guilt.

- **Overeating or Unhealthy Eating.** Poor dietary choices can negatively impact our physical and mental health.

- **Sedentary Lifestyle.** Lack of physical activity can lead to health problems and decreased energy levels.

- **Negative Self-Talk.** Constantly criticizing ourselves can damage our self-esteem and well-being.

- **Excessive Screen Time.** Spending too much time on devices can interfere with sleep, relationships, and productivity.

Breaking Negative Habits

Breaking negative habits can be challenging, but it's entirely possible with the right strategies. Here's how you can start:

- **Identify the Habit Loop.** First, identify the trigger, routine, and reward associated with the negative habit. For example, if you tend to snack unhealthily when stressed, the trigger might be stress, the routine is snacking, and the reward is temporary relief from stress.

- **Replace the Routine.** Instead of trying to eliminate the eating habit altogether, replace the negative routine with a positive one that provides a similar reward. For instance, if stress triggers unhealthy snacking, try replacing the snack with a healthier option or engaging in a stress-relief activity like a quick walk or deep breathing exercises.

- **Modify the Environment.** Make changes to your environment that support the new behavior. If you're trying to eat healthier, keep nutritious snacks readily available and remove junk food from your home. If you want to reduce screen time, designate tech-free zones or times in your day.

- **Start Small.** Small, incremental changes are more sustainable than drastic overhauls. Focus on one habit at a time and break it down into manageable steps. If you're trying to start a daily exercise routine, begin with a short walk and gradually increase the duration and intensity.

- **Use Positive Reinforcement.** Reward yourself for making progress. Positive reinforcement can help solidify new habits. Celebrate your successes, no matter how small, to stay motivated and build momentum.

- **Seek Support.** Having a support system can make a significant difference. Share the habits you're changing with friends or family, join a group with like-minded people, or seek guidance from a coach or therapist. And consider getting an accountability partner—someone who'll cheer you on and help keep you on track.

Building Empowering Habits

Building empowering habits follows a similar process. Here are some tips to help you cultivate positive behaviors:

- **Set Clear Outcomes.** Define what you want to achieve with your new habit. Clear, specific outcomes provide direction and purpose. Instead of saying, "I want to read more," set an outcome to read for 20 minutes every day.

- **Create a Routine.** Establish a consistent routine to incorporate the new habit into your daily life. Consistency helps reinforce the behavior and make it automatic. For example, if you want to start meditating, choose a specific time and place each day to practice.

- **Track Your Progress.** Keep a record of your efforts and achievements. Tracking progress helps you stay motivated and identify patterns that work. Use a journal, app, or calendar to log your activities and reflect on your journey.

- **Stay Flexible.** Life is unpredictable, and it's essential to be adaptable. If you miss a day or encounter setbacks, don't get discouraged. Adjust your plan as needed and keep moving forward. Progress is more important than perfection.

- **Visualize Success.** Visualization can be a powerful tool. Imagine yourself successfully engaging in the new habit and experiencing the benefits. Visualization reinforces positive outcomes and strengthens your commitment to change.

- **Practice Patience.** Building new habits takes time. Be patient with yourself and trust the process. Celebrate small victories along the way and remind yourself that lasting change is a gradual journey.

Here's a high five for taking the first step! You've just unlocked the secret weapon of high achievers: the power of habit transformation. Remember, change takes time and grace. Celebrate every victory, no matter how small, because each one brings you closer to living the life you dream of.

Now, get out there and start experimenting! What small, positive habit can you begin building? It could be anything—a morning meditation, writing in your journal, or even a power walk around the block.

Every step counts on your journey to LIVE BIG!

Mental Habits: How to Create Mindset Magic

Up until now, we've been talking about physical habits, but it's a mind-body adventure when you LIVE BIG. And our thoughts play a massive role in how we experience the world.

How often do little things throw you off? Maybe it's the dishes piled high in the sink, or that one family member who seems to have a talent for leaving the toilet seat up (no judgment here!). These tiny annoyances can quickly spiral into frustration, dragging down your mood and zapping your energy.

Here's the good news: you have the power to shift these negative patterns! We can learn to **reframe** those disempowering mental habits, the very thoughts that drag us down and zap our joy. Think of it like mental jujitsu—flipping negativity on its head and using its energy to fuel our awesomeness.

How to Become a Reframing Rock Star

The secret weapon? Awareness. Throughout your day, catch yourself when Grumpy Greg starts opening the cage door or unhelpful behaviors start creeping in. Maybe you find yourself dwelling on negative self-talk. That's your cue to hit the pause button and ask yourself some powerful questions: "What's the positive side of this? How can I use this to grow and feel empowered?"

By seeking out the positive spin, you transform a potential pit stop into a stepping stone. The more you practice this, the stronger your "reframing muscles" become. Shifting into a positive mindset isn't about pretending everything is sunshine and rainbows, it's about taking control of your thoughts and choosing how you want to react.

Maybe your cluttered garage reminds you it's time to delegate chores (hello, family meeting time!). Or instead of fuming over the toilet seat situation, you reframe it as a playful reminder to practice patience. You might be surprised at how a little perspective shift can empower you to tackle any challenge.

Confession Time

This morning, I walked into the kitchen and saw a mountain of dirty dishes waiting for me, and almost immediately, Grumpy Greg busted out of his cage with thoughts like, "Why am I always the one cleaning up? Can't anyone else pitch in around here?"

Now, even though I know how to manage my mindset, I'm not perfect at it all the time. And guess what? That's totally okay. The goal isn't perfection. We're all works in progress, myself included!

It's about being aware of those slip-ups and catching them before they steal your sunshine.

Here's how I look at it: when you see that storm cloud forming in your mind, grab your mental umbrella and reframe the situation. With a quick shift in perspective, those dishes turned into the perfect excuse to pop in my headphones, crank up an audiobook, and fuel my mind while loading the dishwasher. That extra dose of knowledge? Total win!

The key is staying aware and flexible. Catch the negativity, flip it with a positive spin, and keep moving forward with your amazing day. We're all in this together, superstars, and a little slip-up is no big deal. Just dust yourself off, give that mental umbrella a shake, and keep on shining!

CHAPTER 13

KNOWLEDGE HACKING, MY FAVORITE LIVE BIG NINJA TRICK

As I shared at the beginning of this book, before hitting the "retired from corporate" button, I had a fancy title on the leadership team of a global consulting firm. It was an incredible learning experience, but the long hours were taking their toll, the stress was a constant companion, and a little voice inside me kept whispering that it was time for a change.

The kicker? That job came with a seriously impressive paycheck, and my family depended on my salary. The thought of leaving that financial stability was terrifying.

But there was a tiny spark of hope—a spark that ultimately became a raging fire (in a good way!). On the side, I'd been dipping my toes into the world of real estate, and I'd just snagged my first two vacation rentals—adorable little condos on the beautiful shores of Myrtle Beach, South Carolina.

I was instantly hooked on my new "Airbnb biz," but the reality of running a 24/7 hospitality operation hit me hard—even with just two properties. As a newbie, I didn't have the know-how to really thrive. Maximizing revenue, screening guests, becoming a Superhost … it all felt overwhelming.

So, I did what any resourceful person would do: I followed Dan Sullivan's *Who Not How* approach and went searching for my "Who"—someone with the time, experience, and expertise I didn't have. Someone with years of short-term rental wisdom that I could plug into my business.

That's when I hired Jessie. She became my *knowledge hack*. (And yep, I coined that term, so don't bother searching for it in Webster's Dictionary!) Jessie took charge of revenue management, guest screening, and pretty much everything related to guests. My role? When a repair popped up, I just coordinated with our maintenance guy. Easy-peasy—I could handle that!

Knowledge hacking is all about tapping into someone else's experience and expertise, so you don't have to figure it all out on your own. It's about getting the right insights from an experienced person—fast!

Why I Love Knowledge Hacking

Imagine bypassing endless videos, books, and seminars. *Knowledge hacking* lets you tap straight into the brain of someone who's already mastered it. It's like skipping "YouTube University" and going directly to a coach or mentor who knows exactly how to help you succeed.

My knowledge hacking wasn't a one-time thing. As my short-term rental portfolio grew, so did the demands—more guest inquiries, more check-ins. Time for another *knowledge hack*! I built a 24/7 concierge team, filling it with former Airbnb customer service reps. They brought their insider knowledge of the platform, and that expertise took our business to the next level!

How Else Has Knowledge Hacking Helped Me?

- Building the largest Facebook group for women in short-term rentals? Yup, a knowledge hack! I joined a coaching program to learn the ropes of running a thriving Facebook group.

- Creating a world-renowned training, mentoring, and mastermind program? Knowledge hack! I hired a coach to teach me how to design a successful program and help me avoid common pitfalls.

- Hosting transformational summits, retreats, and events? Knowledge hack! I brought on project management and event planning experts to help me navigate all the details.

See the pattern? I have the vision for the outcome I want to achieve, I build a strategy, and then I find someone with the experience and expertise *I* don't have to help me execute. This knowledge hacking approach fast-tracks your results and saves you from overwhelm because you've got an expert by your side.

Think of Elon Musk launching a rocket. Does he design every part himself, or does he assemble teams of expert engineers to ensure it reaches orbit?

Knowledge hacking is about bringing in the right people to help you reach new heights quickly and efficiently, so you can focus on your vision and get there faster.

Why Knowledge Hacking Is Awesome

- **Transform Years Into Days.** Condense years of trial and error into just days when you have the right people around you.

- **Skip the Heartache.** We've all faced those tough lessons. With knowledge hacking, you're tapping into someone else's experience to dodge the same mistakes.

- **Targeted Learning.** Knowledge hacking gives you guidance from someone who's already conquered your challenge, so you can take action confidently!

How to Become a Knowledge Hacker

There are many ways to tap into the brains of amazing people; here are three of my faves!

- **Hire a Knowledge Powerhouse.** Imagine a dream come true: someone with the experience you crave, working on your team. This is exactly what I did when I built my short-term rental business. While juggling a busy W-2 job, I didn't have the time to figure out all the hosting details on my own. So, I brought in an expert to fast-track my success. It was a game-changer.

- **Join a Coaching Program or Mastermind.** These programs give you direct access to the leader's expertise, help you sidestep costly mistakes, and allow you to learn from the experiences of others on the same journey. It's an investment I wholeheartedly believe in—it's knowledge that can deliver results and pay dividends for years to come.

- **Bring On a Consultant or Advisor.** Need a more personalized approach? A consultant or advisor can be your secret weapon. They can offer guidance, do specific tasks, or even create a custom roadmap to your goals. This option gives you flexibility and ensures you get exactly the support you need.

Knowledge hacking isn't about replacing books, podcasts, or training. It's about strategically adding a powerful tool to your tool belt. By leveraging the wisdom of those who've gone before you, you can accelerate achievement of your desired outcomes.

Knowledge is power, but the *right* knowledge, delivered at the *right* time, is what unlocks the kind of results that you can take straight to the bank.

The Cost of Knowledge Hacking

Let's face it, knowledge hacking isn't free. You're investing in yourself, your business, and your future. But here's the truth—the return on investment can be massive. And the cost of lost opportunities and mistakes? That's even higher.

Here's what knowledge hacking helps you avoid:

- **Lost Opportunity.** Time is your most valuable resource. While you're spinning your wheels trying to figure it all out, someone with the right expertise could already be helping you see results.

- **Costly Mistakes.** Trial and error can cost you—big time. You might waste time, money, and energy on the wrong moves before finding the right path.

- **Overwhelm.** Information overload is real. Drowning in a sea of conflicting opinions from internet gurus can leave you feeling stuck and paralyzed, making it harder to move forward and slowing down your progress.

For me, the choice is clear. I'd rather invest in myself and hack my way to the top. The return on investment is just too big to ignore.

And, I want to be clear, knowledge hacking isn't about skipping learning altogether. You learn by diving in and doing, with an experienced guide by your side to help you navigate each step. This accelerates your momentum, and soon enough, your Dream Seeds start growing faster than ever.

So the next time you're staring down a big goal, don't hesitate to find your knowledge hack—someone who can turn decades into days for you. My favorite question to ask myself is, "Who's my who?"

With the right folks in your corner, you'll be amazed at how quickly you can progress. Surround yourself with the right team, and watch as your dreams transform into reality!

CHARTING YOUR BIGGEST ADVENTURE YET!

We've reached the final chapter of this incredible journey together, and girl—you've covered some serious ground! You've learned how to Boss² Up and grow your Garden of Dreams. You've unlocked how your mind works, picked up powerful tools to master your mindset, learned how to unleash your inner badass, and know how to take charge of your future.

But guess what? This is just the beginning! Think of this book as your launchpad, catapulting you toward a life brimming with possibility and purpose.

Now, I know what you might be thinking, "Okay, Stacey, this has all been amazing, but where do I go from here?"

Here's the beautiful truth: the power is *in your hands*. With this book, you've equipped yourself with a toolbox full of practical tips, powerful strategies, and a brand-new mindset. The next step? Unlock that toolbox and start building your dream life—brick by beautiful brick.

Remember, every small step is a step toward the BIG life you're destined for. You already have everything inside of you to create a life that truly lights you up, so go ahead and make it happen! The best is yet to come.

Here's your action plan to implement LIVE BIG in your life:

1. **Don't Let the Book Become a Bookend.** This book isn't meant to be a one-time read and then forgotten on a dusty shelf. Keep it handy! Refer back to the chapters that resonate with you and use the tools and exercises provided to stay on track. And don't forget to celebrate your progress.

2. **Become a Master of Implementation.** Knowledge without action is like a delicious recipe that never gets cooked. Start implementing the strategies you've learned! Set small, achievable goals, track your progress, and celebrate every victory, big or small. One of the best tools to help you stay on track is the **LIVE BIG 90-Day Momentum Maker.** Grab your copy now at **LiveBigWithStacey. com/momentum** and watch your Garden of Dreams bloom faster than you thought possible!

3. **Embrace the Journey.** This is a marathon, not a sprint, my friend. There will be bumps along the way, moments of doubt, and days when Boss^{2}ing Up feels like a serious uphill climb. And that's okay! Give yourself grace, learn from your setbacks, and keep moving forward. Remember, even the most successful people have their tough days— myself included!

4. **Fuel Your Fire.** Stay connected to the inspiration that brought you here! Visit **LiveBigWithStacey.com** for additional resources, tips, and news about upcoming LIVE BIG events.

Most importantly, never forget the incredible person you are. You've got the power to achieve amazing things, to create a life that lights you up, and to build a business that turns your passions into paychecks.

So, Boss² Up, Show Up for yourself, make those tough decisions with confidence, and Step Up into your best life. The world needs your unique spark, your big dreams, and your unstoppable spirit.

Yes, it's time—time for you to LIVE BIG!

IGNITE THE RIPPLE EFFECT—
SHARE YOUR JOURNEY &
INSPIRE OTHERS

We've come a long way together on this LIVE BIG journey. You've dug deep and unearthed your wildest dreams. You now understand the power of your mind, and here you stand, poised to transform your dreams into a reality that explodes with color and purpose.

Remember, achieving your dreams and living your best life isn't just about you. It's about the ripple effect you create. Imagine the impact you can have by sharing the knowledge you've gained with someone you love—a friend, a family member, any woman with a business dream who yearns to break free from the ordinary and live a life that ignites her soul.

Think about it—by simply passing on this book, you can be the spark that ignites her own personal revolution. Imagine the power of brainstorming, sharing wins (and yes, even those inevitable setbacks) with a sister by your side. The support, the camaraderie ... it can make all the difference on your journey toward Living BIG.

May I ask a quick favor? If you haven't already posted a review, would you take a minute to share one? Your story could be the spark that lights up someone else's path. And leaving an online review is simple:

1. Head to the page or wherever you purchased the book.
2. Scroll down to "Customer Reviews" and click "Write a customer review."
3. Share your honest feedback, and hit submit!

Last but certainly not least, I'd *love* to hear from you! Your voice matters, and by sharing your experience, you could inspire and uplift others on their own journey.

If you're feeling especially bold, post a picture of yourself holding a copy of the *LIVE BIG* book and tag me online. Share your biggest takeaway from the book with everyone to help spread the LIVE BIG message.

Together, we're building a community of like-minded women who are stepping into and living their fullest potential. The world needs more people living with purpose and joy, and I'm beyond grateful to have you as part of this movement.

With love and excitement,

Stacey

ACKNOWLEDGMENTS

To my amazing husband, Chad, and my incredible kiddos, Hayden and Brendan. You are my rock, my heart, and my biggest supporters. Thank you for standing by me every step of the way. I love you more than words could ever express!

To Lauryn—my right hand, right arm, right hip ... basically the other half of me! You're not just the best support anyone could ask for, but a trusted friend through and through. Thank you for always having my back and for being such a huge part of my journey.

To my incredible team—Jessie, Carrie, AJ, Patrick, Febz, Muysen, Pat, Yash, Chelsey, Lace, Kris, Janice, Alicia, and Karey. I couldn't have done this without you. Your daily support gave me the space to write this book, and I appreciate each and every one of you more than you know!

To the incredible women inside my STR Success Accelerator. You're the reason this book exists. Your stories pushed me to put all these thoughts on paper—without you, this info would still be bottled up in my head. Thank you for being the driving force behind this project!

To my wonderful book editing and production team, Lori Lynn— I'm so grateful Michelle recommended you. Your guidance, suggestions, and hard work made this process so much smoother. BIG thanks to you and Kathy Haskins for all your polish and shine! And to Shanda Trofe and the rock stars at Transcendent Publishing, your creativity and guidance have been nothing short of fabulous. Thank you from the bottom of my heart!

And, last but certainly not least, thank you to my amazing parents. Mom, you left this earth far too soon, but I know you're with me every single day, guiding me. Dad, you are the epitome of love, leadership, and hard work—thank you for the opportunity to learn from you. I'm proud to be your daughter. And Linda, thank you for bringing love back into Dad's life after Mom passed, and for being the best bonus mom I could have asked for.

ABOUT THE AUTHOR

Stacey St. John started investing in real estate by accident in 2018, bought her first short-term rental in 2020 (she actually bought two at the same time), and turned $50,000 into a $2 million portfolio in two years.

In March of 2020, she started the Female Short-Term Rental Investors Facebook group, which now has more than 60,000 members worldwide who eat, sleep, breathe, and chat about short-term rentals every day.

She runs the #1 training, mentoring, and mastermind program exclusively for women in the short-term rental industry. Her podcast, *The STR Sisterhood*, has been named an industry favorite several times.

She's sung in two world championship a cappella quartets (2009 and 2024) and has the honor of being named in the 2009 *Guinness Book of World Records* for giving the world's largest singing lesson.

When she's not building her business or helping other women build theirs, she enjoys binge-watching *Shark Tank* with a glass of red wine, laughing with her friends and family, and traveling to the beach to watch sunrises over the ocean.

She's passionate about helping people understand and unlock their potential. In her opinion, there is no greater reward than to impact the lives of others in a positive way.

Originally a small-town girl from Columbus, Indiana, Stacey now resides in Cincinnati, Ohio, with her husband, Chad, and their chihuahua, Chi Chi, the loudest three pounds you'll ever meet. They are the proud parents of two adult sons, Hayden and Brendan. The same year she wrote this book, she and her beloved "Chadder" celebrated their 30th wedding anniversary.

HOW TO ACCESS YOUR
LIVE BIG RESOURCES

Throughout this book, you've discovered powerful strategies, tools, and tactics to help you Boss^2 Up, Show Up, and Step Up into your dream life.

Now, it's time to put them into action!

Head over to **LiveBigWithStacey.com/resources** (or scan the QR code below) to download all the resources I've included in this book.

And don't forget to check back regularly because I'm constantly updating the site with fresh content designed to help you keep moving forward and Living BIG!

LiveBigWithStacey.com/resources

WHICH ZONE ARE YOU IN?

As we wrap up this book, I want to leave you with one final, powerful tool for your toolkit—one that will help you identify the zone you're operating in and make sure you're on track to LIVE BIG.

Did you know that entrepreneurs move through four distinct zones on their journey to success? These are the Comfort Zone, the Fear Zone, the Learning Zone, and the BIG Zone.

Each one comes with its own unique challenges and opportunities. If you don't know which zone you're in, it's hard to know which next steps you should take.

Are you ready to find out which zone you're operating from?

Take my quick, two-minute LIVE BIG quiz to discover your current zone. Whether you're hanging out in your Comfort Zone, feeling stuck in the Fear Zone, embracing growth in the Learning Zone, or thriving in the BIG Zone, this quiz will give you the clarity you need to level up.

Uncover the truth about where you are now, and let's make sure you're on the path to where you want to be. It's time to LIVE BIG—both in your life *and* your business.

Take the quiz now and get ready to step into your BIG Zone!

LiveBigWithStacey.com/quiz